100-CALORIE SNACK COOKBOOK

100-CALORIE SNACK COOKBOOK

SALLY SAMPSON

FOREWORD BY KATHY McMANUS, M.S., R.D.

PHOTOGRAPHY BY CARL TREMBLAY

JOHN WILEY & SONS

Copyright © 2009 by Sally Sampson. All rights reserved
Photography copyright 2009 by Carl Tremblay
Foreword copyright 2009 by Katherine D. McManus, M.S., R.D.

Published by John Wiley & Sons, Inc., Hoboken, New Jersey
Published simultaneously in Canada

For general information on our other products and services or for technical support, please contact our Customer Care Department within the United States at (800) 762-2974, outside the United States at (317) 572-3993 or fax (317) 572-4002.

Wiley also publishes its books in a variety of electronic formats. Some content that appears in print may not be available in electronic books. For more information about Wiley products, visit our web site at www.wiley.com.

Book design by Elizabeth Van Itallie

Library of Congress Cataloging-in-Publication Data:
Sampson, Sally, 1955-
    100-calorie snack cookbook / Sally Sampson ; foreword by Katherine D. McManus ; photography by Carl Tremblay.
        p. cm.
    Includes index.
    ISBN 978-0-470-45198-4 (pbk.)
    1. Low-calorie diet--Recipes. 2. Snack foods. I. Title. II. Title: One hundred calorie snack cookbook.
    RM222.2.S237 2009
    641.5'635--dc22
                                                    2008044732

Printed in the United States of America

10 9 8 7 6 5 4 3 2

FOR LAUREN AND BEN,
WITHOUT WHOM
IT WOULDN'T MATTER

ACKNOWLEDGMENTS

Love and thanks to Susan Orlean, who fed me the idea;
to Justin Schwartz, Jana Nordstrand, Christine DiComo, Carla Glasser
and Jenny Alperen, because little happens without them;
and to Carl Tremblay, for his gorgeous photographs and patience.

CONTENTS

FOREWORD

Despite widespread interest in weight and weight control, the prevalence of obesity continues to rise in the United States and worldwide. There have been various studies that reported examining the risk and benefits of snacking between meals. Snacking for most individuals appears not to adversely affect weight control and for some it may improve control. This improvement may occur because frequent eating helps appetite control, thus preventing overeating at meals.

The main question then is what kind of snack and how much? With the plethora of readily available, highly processed, packaged snack foods, it can be difficult to make the right choice.

Sally Sampson's *100-Calorie Snack Cookbook* is the perfect answer to the dilemma. This cookbook offers more than two hundred recipes that are only 100 calories, free of trans fat, low in saturated fat, low to moderate in sodium and most importantly great tasting! The author has created an amazing variety of snacks that can meet anyone's craving for sweet, crunchy, savory or just plain delicious. She has taken the unique approach of offering snacks that encompass all the food groups and expertly combines ingredients for fabulous tasting soups, salads, vegetables, eggs, grains, desserts, beverages and more, in only 100 calories per serving! Snacking no longer needs to be boring or unhealthy. These fantastic snack ideas can help improve the quality of your daily food intake, serve as a great energizer to keep you going throughout the day and potentially help you reach or maintain a healthy weight.

—KATHY McMANUS, M.S., R.D.
Director, Department of Nutrition
Brigham and Women's Hospital
A teaching affiliate of Harvard Medical School

INTRODUCTION

Are you trying to lose weight? Or simply hoping not to gain any? Do you drink a protein shake for breakfast, eat a salad for lunch and grilled fish for dinner? Do you dine on low-fat soups and lean chicken? Are you "good" at meals but not-so-good in between? Do you crave low-fat pretzels, only to eat half the bag, telling yourself after each that it's your last? Do you hit the wall after coming in from a long run and stand in front of the fridge scarfing down all you can find, only to have consumed all your recommended daily allowances? Are you suffering from a devastating break-up and find yourself popping chocolate bon-bons?

Whether you are on a diet of your own making, Weight Watchers, the Atkins Diet, the Scarsdale Diet, the Cookie Diet, the Grapefruit Diet, the Cabbage Soup Diet, the South Beach Diet, the Low-Carb, Low-Fat or High-Protein Diet, other than exercising, weight loss comes down to one thing.

Calories.

And honestly, even if you aren't on a diet, no doubt you want to maintain your weight and get through the day feeling satiated and energized rather than stuffed and depleted. If you want to lose weight, whether it's 2 pounds or 200 pounds, the best way to accomplish it is to take in fewer calories, which means eating smaller servings and smaller snacks—and current research tells us that 100 is the magic caloric number for snacking. It's that simple.

But do you know what constitutes 100 calories?

Peaches 'n' Cream, page 201

Just wander, as I did, around a grocery store and note the proliferation of 100-calorie snacks: this aisle is getting more and more crowded every day and since I started tracking this trend, the bounty has at least doubled.

But not everyone, certainly not I, wants a ridiculously expensive, wastefully overpackaged snack loaded with chemicals, sugar and salt, a snack designed to sit on a grocery store shelf for a year, if not two. I don't want to eat it and I surely don't want to feed it to my kids. And neither do you.

But do you want to spend all your time counting calories? I doubt it. So I saved you the trouble and did it for you! This book is filled with everything I could think of: no-brainer snacks, soups, easy salads and slightly more complicated salads, a few egg dishes and mini-meals, beverages, recipes for bags of Gorp to stick in your kids' backpacks and foods you wouldn't dream of eating when you're paying attention to calories: treats like chocolate truffles and caramels. This jam-packed little book will be so indispensa-
ble, you'll need one copy for home and another for work. You might even need one for the car.

The *100-Calorie Snack Cookbook* will help you head off hunger and indulge without taking in too many calories. Armed with these ideas and recipes, you won't spend your whole day with a growling stomach, and even though you'll be snacking, you won't have that awful feeling of being naughty. You'll no longer feel bad physically (all that sugar! all that salt!) and bad about yourself too ("why didn't I eat something better?" you ask yourself). Just as you want to avoid the grocery store when you're hungry, if you want control over your eating, it is essential to be prepared with healthy, satisfying, 100-calorie choices.

Roasted Chickpeas, page 65

Filled with ideas for no-cook snacks, the *100-Calorie Snack Cookbook* includes recipes that can be made easily, whether you only have five minutes in the morning, or a few more when you get home from work.

ON CALORIES

When calculating the calories for this book, I endeavored to be as accurate as possible. However, unless I am in your kitchen watching your every move—in fact, unless I go with you to the grocery store or am actually manufacturing the item myself—it's hard to be exact. One can of tuna is not necessarily the same as another can of tuna, even if they are both white and packed in water. One apple is surely not the same as any other, even if both are Granny Smiths. All chocolate chips are not created equal. Even measuring spoons and cups vary. So understand that these calorie counts are guidelines and be mindful of your ingredients and remember, if a recipe calls for a medium-size ingredient and you use an extra large one, it's okay as long as you aren't kidding yourself!

SOUPS

BORSCHT
SERVES 6, ABOUT 2 CUPS PER SERVING

E ven if you don't like beets, it's worth making borscht, the classic chilled soup, just to eye its stunning, deep pink color. Seriously though, if you are a beet detractor you probably haven't yet had good borscht or properly cooked beets. Although they are most commonly discarded, I like to include the beet greens when making borscht; they are high in iron, folate, potassium and a variety of B vitamins.

6 cups sliced or chopped cooked beets
6 cups beet liquid
4 cups beet greens
½ cup plain nonfat buttermilk
1 teaspoon kosher salt
Juice of 1 lemon
Fresh dill leaves
½ cup plain low-fat yogurt, for garnish
  (optional)

■ Place the beets and 2 cups beet liquid in a blender and blend until well chopped. Add another cup liquid and blend again. Remove half the mixture to a bowl. Add the beet greens and remaining beet liquid and puree until smooth. Remove half again and add to the bowl. Add the buttermilk, salt and lemon juice and puree again. Pour the remaining beet mixture into the bowl, cover and refrigerate until chilled, at least 2 hours and up to 3 days. Serve garnished with the dill and additional yogurt, if desired.

NUTRITION FACTS: Calories: 97; Calories from Fat: 7; Fat: 0.8g; Saturated Fat: 0g; Cholesterol: 2mg; Sodium: 554mg; Carbohydrates: 19.8g; Dietary Fiber: 3.4g; Protein: 4.6g

GINGER MELON SOUP

SERVES 4, ABOUT 2 CUPS PER SERVING

Low in calories, high in fiber, water and air, melons help control your appetite by filling you up. Research shows that when water is contained in the food you eat, as opposed to being consumed alongside it, you fill up more readily, which, in turn, makes you eat less. Although I generally like to eat most melons alone (or less often, wrapped in prosciutto) I make an exception for this sweet juicy soup!

- ½ cantaloupe, peeled, seeded and chopped
- ½ honeydew melon, peeled, seeded and chopped
- ⅞ cup plain low-fat yogurt
- 1½ tablespoons peeled, finely chopped fresh gingerroot
- 1 tablespoon fresh lime juice
- 1 teaspoon freshly grated lime zest
- Fresh mint leaves

■ Place all the ingredients except the mint leaves in the bowl of a food processor fitted with a steel blade, and process until smooth. Transfer to a container, cover and refrigerate for at least 1 hour and up to 4. Serve garnished with the mint.

NUTRITION FACTS: Calories: 100; Calories from Fat: 10; Fat: 1.1g; Saturated Fat: 0.6g; Cholesterol: 3mg; Sodium: 69mg; Carbohydrates: 20.5g; Dietary Fiber: 1.5g; Protein: 3.9g

CHICKEN SOUP WITH LEMON ZEST AND FRESH THYME

SERVES 6, ABOUT 2 CUPS PER SERVING

Grandma's chicken soup with a twist. Literally.

1 small onion, coarsely chopped
3 carrots, halved lengthwise and thinly sliced
2 celery stalks, halved lengthwise and sliced
10 cups low-sodium chicken stock
1 bay leaf
Freshly grated zest of ½ lemon, or more to taste
1½ cups shredded or diced cooked chicken
1 tablespoon fresh thyme leaves

■ Place the onion, carrots, celery and ¼ cup stock in a large stockpot over medium heat and cook until the vegetables are tender, 10 to 15 minutes. Add the remaining stock and bay leaf and cook over low heat for 1 hour.
■ Add the lemon zest, chicken and thyme and serve or cover and refrigerate for up to 3 days.

NUTRITION FACTS: Calories: 97; Calories from Fat: 11; Fat: 1.2g; Saturated Fat: 0g; Cholesterol: 27mg; Sodium: 165mg; Carbohydrates: 6.1g; Dietary Fiber: 1.3g; Protein: 14g

GAZPACHO

SERVES 5, ABOUT 2 CUPS PER SERVING

The perfect summer cooler, gazpacho is packed with lush summer produce: cucumbers, tomatoes and bell peppers make it light, invigorating and yet substantial. Refrigerate gazpacho in small containers for a great between-meal snack or combine two portions for a heartier lunch.

2 small English cucumbers, diced
2 beefsteak or other large tomatoes, cored and diced
1 small red onion, coarsely chopped
2 garlic cloves, minced
2 red bell peppers, cored, seeded and coarsely chopped
1 tablespoon sherry or red wine vinegar
3½ cups low-sodium tomato or V8 juice
1 cup water
⅓ cup chopped fresh dill, cilantro or basil leaves (optional)
¼ cup feta cheese, crumbled

■ Place the cucumbers, tomatoes, onion, garlic and peppers in a bowl and toss to combine. Remove half the mixture and place in the bowl of a food processor fitted with a steel blade and pulse 2 to 3 times until chopped and combined. Return to the bowl.
■ Add the vinegar, tomato juice and water and stir to combine.
■ Cover and refrigerate for at least 2 hours and up to overnight. Serve garnished with additional herbs, if desired, and feta.

NUTRITION FACTS: Calories: 103; Calories from Fat: 19; Fat: 2.1g; Saturated Fat: 1.2g; Cholesterol: 7mg; Sodium: 110mg; Carbohydrates: 19.4g; Dietary Fiber: 3.4g; Protein: 4.5g

CILANTRO GAZPACHO

SERVES 2, ABOUT 2 CUPS PER SERVING

Gazpacho for cilantro lovers! This version of gazpacho forgoes tomatoes and adds a healthy dose of cilantro, the leaf of the coriander plant. Traditionally found in Asian, Caribbean and Latin American cuisines, people either love or detest cilantro: to those who hate it, its fragrance is deemed sweaty and its flavor soapy. To the rest of us, its distinctive flavor is divine.

- 1 green, yellow or orange bell pepper, cored, seeded and diced
- 1 English cucumber, diced
- 2 garlic cloves, minced
- 1 orange, peeled, pitted and chopped
- 1 small bunch scallions, green and white parts or 1 small red onion, chopped
- 2 tablespoons chopped fresh cilantro leaves
- 1 cup ice cubes or water
- ½ teaspoon black pepper
- 1 jalapeño pepper, seeded, if desired, and finely chopped (optional)

■ Place the bell pepper, cucumber, garlic, orange, scallions and cilantro in a large bowl. Transfer half the mixture to a food processor and pulse to chop. Add the ice cubes and pulse again. Return the mixture to the bowl and stir well. Add the pepper and, if desired, the jalapeño. Cover and refrigerate for at least 2 hours and up to overnight.

NUTRITION FACTS: Calories: 92; Calories from Fat: 5; Fat: 0.5g; Saturated Fat: 0g; Cholesterol: 0mg; Sodium: 10mg; Carbohydrates: 21.6g; Dietary Fiber: 4.6g; Protein: 2.8g

KEEP IN MIND

1 tablespoon mayonnaise = 90 calories
1 tablespoon honey = 58 calories
1 tablespoon real maple syrup = 52 calories
1 teaspoon olive (and almost all other) oil = 40 calories
1 teaspoon unsalted butter = 40 calories
1 tablespoon brown sugar = 35 calories
1 tablespoon white sugar = 25 calories
1 tablespoon ketchup = 15 calories
1 tablespoon soy sauce = 10 calories
1 tablespoon balsamic vinegar = 10 calories
1 teaspoon Dijon mustard = 5 calories
1 tablespoon capers = 5 calories
1 teaspoon Sriracha hot chili sauce = 5 calories
6 cornichons = 5 calories
1 teaspoon yellow mustard = 0 calories
1 tablespoon rice wine vinegar = 0 calories
1 tablespoon sherry vinegar = 0 calories
1 tablespoon red wine vinegar = 0 calories
1 teaspoon Tuong Ot Toi Viet-Nam Chili Garlic Sauce = 0 calories
1 teaspoon horseradish = 0 calories
1 teaspoon Tabasco = 0 calories
1 teaspoon Worcestershire = 0 calories

BROCCOLI SOUP WITH LEMON AND YOGURT
SERVES 5, ABOUT 2 CUPS PER SERVING

B roccoli soup is so often overcooked in restaurants I never order it. However, I like almost all homemade renditions, particularly this slightly tart chilled version. Broccoli is a nutrition super-star: high in cancer-fighting antioxidants, fiber, potassium, calcium, vitamin C, lutein and zeax-anthin (good for eyes) and relatively high in protein (for a vegetable). Be sure to use the stalks and the greens, which hold lots of flavor and nutrients.

1 teaspoon olive oil
1 Spanish onion, coarsely chopped
1 celery stalk, chopped
1 small carrot, sliced
6 cups low-sodium chicken stock
1 head broccoli, including the leaves, woody stems discarded, florets and remaining stems chopped
Juice and freshly grated zest of 1 lemon
½ cup plain low-fat yogurt
Kosher salt and black pepper

▓ Place a 4-quart soup pot over medium heat and when it is hot, add the oil. Add the onion, celery and carrot and cook until tender, 10 to 15 minutes.
▓ Add the chicken stock, raise the heat to high and bring to a boil. While the soup is boiling, slowly add the broccoli florets. Return to a boil briefly. Reduce the heat to medium and cook until the broccoli is just tender, 5 to 8 minutes.
▓ Remove the solids and place them in a food processor or blender. Process until smooth, gradually adding the liquid. Add additional stock if the soup is too thick. Transfer to a lidded container and refrigerate until chilled, about 2 hours.
▓ Just prior to serving, add the lemon juice and zest and the yogurt. Add salt and pepper to taste.

NUTRITION FACTS: Calories: 96; Calories from Fat: 16; Fat: 1.8g; Saturated Fat: 0g; Cholesterol: 1mg; Sodium: 152mg; Carbohydrates: 14.1g; Dietary Fiber: 3.9g; Protein: 7.5g

TOMATO CUCUMBER SOUP WITH YOGURT

SERVES 4, ABOUT 1¾ CUPS PER SERVING

've been making tomato cucumber soup for over twenty years and I never tire of it: the creamy yogurt mellows the acidity of the tomato juice netting a bright, revitalizing summertime soup.

5 cups tomato or V8 juice
2 tablespoons lemon juice or red wine vinegar
2 to 3 teaspoons curry powder
¼ cup chopped fresh Italian flat-leaf parsley leaves, plus additional for garnish
1¼ cups plain low-fat yogurt
1 English cucumber, quartered lengthwise and finely sliced

■ Place everything except the cucumber in a blender and blend until smooth. Transfer to a bowl, add the cucumbers, cover and refrigerate for at least 2 hours and up to overnight. Serve garnished with additional parsley.

NUTRITION FACTS: Calories: 90; Calories from Fat: 14; Fat: 1.6g; Saturated Fat: 0.7g; Cholesterol: 4mg; Sodium: 56mg; Carbohydrates: 15.8g; Dietary Fiber: 3.1g; Protein: 5.6g

MINESTRONE
SERVES 8, ABOUT 1¾ CUPS PER SERVING

A humble Italian soup composed of fresh, seasonal vegetables (not a repository for leftovers), minestrone often includes beans, pasta and meat, usually chicken or beef. In the fall and winter, minestrone is most always in my fridge, never as a starter (it's too hearty) but rather as a main course—with salad—or an afternoon snack.

1 teaspoon olive or canola oil
1 Spanish onion, finely chopped
2 garlic cloves, pressed or finely chopped
2 celery stalks, peeled and sliced
2 carrots, peeled, quartered lengthwise and sliced
2 teaspoons dried basil
2 zucchini, quartered lengthwise and sliced
2 cups canned or fresh diced tomatoes
10 cups low-sodium chicken stock
½ cup white rice
½ cup cooked or canned dark red kidney beans,
    drained and rinsed
1 Parmesan cheese rind, about 5 inches
Kosher salt and pepper
¼ cup chopped fresh basil leaves

■ Place a stockpot over medium heat and when it is hot, add the oil. Add the onion, garlic, celery, carrots and dried basil and cook, covered, until the vegetables are tender, 10 to 15 minutes.

■ Add the zucchini, tomatoes, stock, rice, beans and Parmesan rind, raise the heat to high and bring just to a boil. Reduce the heat to low and cook, partially covered, for 2 hours.

■ Transfer to a container, cover and refrigerate at least overnight and up to 2 days. Remove and discard the Parmesan cheese rind. Place the soup in a pot and gently reheat. Add salt and pepper to taste. Garnish with the fresh basil.

NUTRITION FACTS: Calories:104, Calories from Fat: 3, Fat: 0.3g; Saturated Fat: 0g; Cholesterol: 0mg; Sodium: 113mg; Carbohydrates: 18g; Dietary Fiber: 2.6g; Protein: 5.6g

MUSHROOM BARLEY SOUP
SERVES 6, ABOUT 1½ CUPS PER SERVING

Almost nut-like in flavor, barley is a grain that provides a variety of nutrients and both depth and bulk to this rich mushroom soup.

1 Spanish onion, chopped
3 garlic cloves, chopped
2 carrots, chopped
1 celery stalk, chopped
1 pound button mushrooms, halved and sliced
½ teaspoon dried thyme
10 cups low-sodium chicken stock
¼ cup barley
½ teaspoon balsamic vinegar or fresh lemon juice
1 tablespoon fresh thyme leaves

■ Place the onion, garlic, carrots, celery, mushrooms, dried thyme and 1 cup chicken stock in a large stockpot and cook, stirring occasionally, until the vegetables have softened, 15 to 20 minutes. Add the remaining chicken stock and barley and bring to a gentle boil. Reduce the heat to low and cook until the barley has softened and the soup starts to come together, about 2 hours. Set aside to cool for 20 minutes.
■ Add the balsamic vinegar and thyme and stir well. Transfer to a container, cover and refrigerate at least overnight and up to 2 days.

NUTRITION FACTS: Calories: 89; Calories from Fat: 5; Fat: 0.6g; Saturated Fat: 0g; Cholesterol: 0mg; Sodium: 139mg; Carbohydrates: 14.4g; Protein: 7.2g.

LENTIL SOUP WITH FRESH MINT, CILANTRO, BASIL AND YOGURT

SERVES 18, ABOUT ¾ CUP PER SERVING

L entil soup is one of my favorite soups to make. Wonderfully nutritious (high in fiber, protein, folate and iron), I feel virtuous eating lentils but almost more importantly I love them for their endless versatility: lentils seem to go with everything. Lentil soup freezes well so make a double batch and freeze it in portion-size containers.

1 teaspoon olive oil
1 Spanish onion, chopped
2 garlic cloves, minced
2 carrots, diced
1 celery stalk, diced
1 tablespoon curry powder
  (hot or sweet)
2 cups brown lentils, washed and
  picked over for pebbles
14 cups low-sodium chicken stock
½ cup plain low-fat yogurt
¼ cup chopped fresh mint leaves
¼ cup chopped fresh cilantro leaves
¼ cup chopped fresh basil leaves

■ Place a large stockpot over medium heat and when it is hot, add the oil. Add the onion, garlic, carrots, celery and curry powder and cook until the onion is soft, about 10 minutes. Add the lentils and chicken stock and bring to a boil. Reduce the heat to low and cook, partially covered, for 2 hours. Cover and refrigerate for up to 5 days or serve, garnished with yogurt and herbs.

NUTRITION FACTS: Calories: 101; Calories from Fat: 6; Fat: 0.7g; Saturated Fat: 0g; Cholesterol: 0mg; Sodium: 59mg; Carbohydrates: 15.9g; Dietary Fiber: 7.2g; Protein: 7.5g

CONGEE (EXPLODED RICE SOUP)

SERVES 8, ABOUT 1 CUP PER SERVING

I had never had congee until my friend, cookbook author Adam Reid, recommended it to my daughter Lauren, who loves rice in almost any form. Congee is a traditional, thick, porridge-like Chinese soup made with rice and is way more appetizing than it sounds. At my house we call it exploded rice soup, because that's basically what happens to the rice!

1 teaspoon canola oil
½ cup diced Spanish onion
½ cup diced carrots
¼ cup diced celery
⅞ cup long grain rice (not parboiled)
8 cups low-sodium chicken stock
½ teaspoon unseasoned rice wine vinegar

ACCOMPANIMENTS (DO NOT PREPARE UNTIL CALLED FOR IN RECIPE)

1 quarter-size piece of fresh gingerroot, minced
4 scallions, including green and white parts, minced
Freshly grated zest of 1 orange
¼ cup chopped fresh cilantro or Italian flat-leaf parsley leaves
1 small jalapeño pepper, seeded, if desired, and minced (optional)

▓ Place a large soup pot over medium heat and when it is hot, add the oil. Add the onion, carrots and celery and cook until softened but not browned, about 10 minutes. Add the rice and chicken stock and bring to a boil. Reduce the heat to low and cook, uncovered, for 30 minutes. Add the vinegar and set aside, covered, while you prepare the accompaniments.
▓ Add the accompaniments just prior to serving.

NUTRITION FACTS: Calories: 103; Calories from Fat: 7; Fat: 0.8g; Saturated Fat: 0g; Cholesterol: 0mg; Sodium: 81mg; Carbohydrates: 19.3; Dietary Fiber: 0.9g; Protein: 3.8g

VIETNAMESE CHICKEN SOUP

SERVES 4, ABOUT 2 CUPS PER SERVING

Although I am a huge fan of the more traditional Americanized chicken soup, there are times when only the Vietnamese version will do. You can eat a huge bowl (about 2 cups) for lunch, dinner or a snack.

2 ounces rice noodles (available at specialty shops)
8 cups low-sodium chicken stock
4 thin slices fresh gingerroot
2 garlic cloves, thinly sliced
1 stalk lemon grass, thinly sliced on the bias
1 teaspoon fish sauce
¾ cup shredded cooked chicken breast
¼ cup chopped fresh cilantro leaves
¼ cup chopped fresh basil leaves
1 cup bean sprouts
Vietnamese chili paste, to taste
1 lime, quartered

■ Place the noodles in a bowl of hot water and let sit until soft, 20 to 30 minutes.
■ Place the stock, gingerroot, garlic and lemon grass in a pot and bring to a boil over high heat. Reduce the heat to low and cook for 20 minutes. Add the fish sauce and cook 5 minutes. Drain the noodles and add to the broth. Add the chicken, cilantro, basil and bean sprouts. Add chili paste and lime to taste.

NUTRITION FACTS: Calories: 105; Calories from Fat: 11; Fat: 1.2g; Saturated Fat: 0g; Cholesterol: 22mg; Sodium: 281mg; Carbohydrates: 8.1g; Dietary Fiber: 0g; Protein: 14.4g

ASPARAGUS SOUP

SERVES 4, ABOUT 2½ CUPS PER SERVING

The woodsy aroma and slightly bittersweet flavor of rosemary melds perfectly with asparagus. Be sure to include the lemon: it brightens them both!

At about 5 calories per stalk, asparagus is very low in calories but blissfully high in vitamins A and C, folic acid, potassium, fiber, vitamin B6, and thiamin.

Refrigerate asparagus as if it were a bouquet of flowers: snip off the outermost woody ends and stand the remainder upright in water.

1 teaspoon olive oil
1 Spanish onion, coarsely chopped
2 garlic cloves, pressed or finely chopped
7 cups low-sodium chicken stock
2½ pounds fresh asparagus, woody stems broken off and discarded, stalks and tips chopped
1 teaspoon fresh rosemary leaves
1 teaspoon fresh lemon juice

▓ Place a 3-quart soup pot over medium heat and when it is hot, add the oil. Add the onion and garlic and cook until tender and lightly colored, 10 to 15 minutes.

▓ Add the chicken stock, raise the heat to high and bring to a boil. Add the asparagus and when it returns to a rolling boil, remove the solids and place them in a blender. Add the rosemary and lemon juice. Process until smooth, gradually adding the liquid. Serve immediately.

NUTRITION FACTS: Calories: 105; Calories from Fat: 14; Fat: 1.5g; Saturated Fat: 0g; Cholesterol: 0mg; Sodium: 129mg; Carbohydrates: 15.6g; Dietary Fiber 6.6g; Protein: 10g

CARROT SOUP WITH CHIVES

SERVES 4, ABOUT 2 CUPS PER SERVING

Chives are the smallest and mildest member of the onion family and while used primarily as a garnish or condiment, I like their inclusion here as a nice counterpoint to the sweetness of the carrots. As a medicinal herb, carrots can be used to lower blood pressure.

1 teaspoon olive oil
1 Spanish onion, coarsely chopped
2 celery stalks, chopped
1 pound carrots, peeled, if desired, and sliced
8 cups low-sodium chicken stock
2 tablespoons fresh chives

■ Place a 3-quart soup pot over medium heat and when it is hot, add the oil. Add the onion, celery and carrots and cook until tender and lightly colored, 10 to 15 minutes. Add the stock, raise the heat to high and bring to a boil. Reduce the heat to low and cook until the carrots are tender, about 20 minutes.

■ Remove the solids and place them in a food processor or blender. Process until smooth, gradually adding the liquid. Transfer to a container, cover and refrigerate for up to 3 days or serve immediately, garnished with the chives.

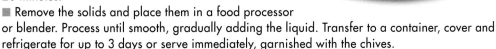

NUTRITION FACTS: Calories: 99; Calories from Fat: 13; Fat: 1.5g; Saturated Fat: 0g; Cholesterol: 0mg; Sodium: 226mg; Carbohydrates: 15.8g; Dietary Fiber: 3.8g; Protein: 5.4g

BLACK BEAN SOUP

SERVES 10, ABOUT ⅔ CUP PER SERVING

I almost didn't include the recipe for this rich, earthy soup because beans are high in calories and this soup takes hours and hours to make. However, black beans are delicious, satisfying and so good for you: high in fiber, manganese, magnesium, phosphorus and thiamin and low in saturated fat and sodium, they have no cholesterol and no sugar. Although I have included the spices that usually make black beans spicy, they are quite mild here: if you like your soup hot and spicy, just increase the spices.

1 large Spanish onion, finely chopped
1 carrot, diced
1 celery stalk, diced
2 garlic cloves, pressed or finely chopped
5½ cups low-sodium chicken stock
1 teaspoon ground cumin
1 teaspoon chili powder
1 teaspoon dried oregano
¼ to ½ teaspoon cayenne pepper
½ pound black turtle beans, soaked
**   overnight, boiled for 1 hour, drained and**
**   rinsed (about 6 cups)**
1 tablespoon fresh lime juice
10 teaspoons plain low-fat yogurt
Chopped fresh cilantro leaves

■ Place the onion, carrot, celery, garlic and 1 cup stock in a heavy-bottomed soup pot or stockpot and bring to a boil over high heat. Reduce the heat to medium and cook until the vegetables are tender, about 10 minutes. Add the cumin, chili powder, oregano and cayenne and cook for 5 minutes. Add the beans and the remaining 4½ cups chicken stock, raise the heat to high, and bring to a boil. Lower the heat to medium and cook, partially covered, stirring frequently, for 2 hours.

■ After 2 hours, check to see if you need to add more stock. If necessary, add 1 to 2 more cups, raise the heat to high and return to a boil. Reduce the heat to low and cook, partially covered, for 2 hours. ■ Cover and refrigerate at least overnight and up to 5 days. Gently reheat over low heat. Serve garnished with lime juice, yogurt and cilantro.

NUTRITION FACTS: Calories: 98; Calories from Fat: 4; Fat: 0.5g; Saturated Fat: 0g; Cholesterol: 0mg; Sodium: 49mg; Carbohydrates: 17.4g; Dietary Fiber: 4.1g; Protein: 6.4g

TOMATO BASIL SOUP WITH CHEDDAR CHEESE

SERVES 6, ABOUT 1¼ CUPS PER SERVING

Rich, creamy and yet very low in calories, tomato basil soup is one of my top favorite soups, in spite of the fact that I am not a fan of cream soups. Do not even think of substituting dried basil for the fresh: fresh basil is essential to this soup. And remember, the word basil comes from the Greek word *basilikos*, or "royal": this soup *is* fit for a king.

1 teaspoon unsalted butter
1 Spanish onion, chopped
1 celery stalk, chopped
1 carrot, sliced
2 garlic cloves, sliced
7 cups diced tomatoes
5 cups low-sodium chicken stock
¼ cup shredded Cheddar cheese
1 tablespoon heavy cream
1 tablespoon balsamic vinegar
½ cup chopped fresh basil leaves, plus additional for garnish

▓ Place a stockpot over medium-high heat and when it is hot, add the butter. When the butter has melted, add the onion, celery, carrot and garlic and cook until tender and lightly colored, 10 to 15 minutes. Add the tomatoes and chicken stock and bring to a boil. Reduce the heat to low and cook, partly covered, for 30 to 45 minutes.
▓ Place a small amount of the soup in a blender and blend until smooth. Add the Cheddar cheese, heavy cream and balsamic vinegar and repeat until all the soup has been blended. Transfer to a container, stir well, cover and refrigerate for up to 3 days or serve immediately, garnished with basil.

NUTRITION FACTS: Calories: 91; Calories from Fat: 32; Fat: 3.5g; Saturated Fat: 2g; Cholesterol: 10mg; Sodium: 119mg; Carbohydrates: 11g; Dietary Fiber: 2.8g; Protein: 4.9g

AVGOLEMONO

SERVES 8, ABOUT 1½ CUPS PER SERVING

A vgolemono, the most popular of Greek soups, is another version of chicken soup. Tart, lemony and hearty, this beautiful yellow soup is thickened with eggs and rice.

12 cups low-sodium chicken stock
½ cup long grain white rice
2 large eggs, at room temperature
2 large egg yolks, at room temperature
⅓ to ½ cup fresh lemon juice
⅓ cup chopped fresh Italian flat-leaf parsley,
   mint or dill leaves

■ Place the chicken stock in a medium-size soup pot and bring to a boil over high heat. Add the rice; reduce the heat to low and cook until the rice is tender, about 15 minutes.

■ Place the eggs, egg yolks and lemon juice in a bowl and whisk together.

■ Very gradually, whisking all the while, add some of the stock to the lemon mixture, being very careful not to let the eggs curdle. Return the mixture to the soup pot and cook over very low heat for 10 minutes. Keep whisking until the stock is combined with the eggs. Serve immediately, garnished with the herbs, or cover and refrigerate for up to 3 days. Gently reheat over low heat.

NUTRITION FACTS: Calories: 104; Calories from Fat: 23; Fat: 2.5g; Saturated Fat: 0.8g; Cholesterol: 105mg; Sodium: 129mg; Carbohydrates: 13g; Protein: 6.5g

EGGS

GREEN EGGS (NO HAM)

SERVES 4

When you prepare these eggs you'll surely think you are doing it wrong: the mixture has the look of all spinach/little egg and doesn't seem as if it will cook properly. But trust me: it will. The combination is great: with only 7 calories per cup, spinach provides calcium, iron and vitamin A. Not only does it improve bone strength, it also improves eyesight and mental functions and helps to prevent against heart disease. It's no wonder it was Popeye's food of choice.

5 large eggs, beaten
**1½ cups tightly packed flat-leaf spinach leaves, finely
  chopped**
**2 scallions, including green and white parts,
  chopped**
¼ teaspoon crushed red pepper flakes
½ teaspoon kosher salt
¼ teaspoon black pepper
1 lime, quartered

■ Place all the ingredients except the lime in a
small bowl and mix well.
■ Place a nonstick pan over medium heat and when
it is hot, add the egg mixture. Cook until the mixture
just starts to set on the sides and then gently flip portions
until the eggs are cooked throughout, but not browned.
Divide into 4 portions and serve immediately, garnished with lime.

NUTRITION FACTS: Calories: 95; Calories from Fat: 57; Fat: 6.3g; Saturated Fat: 2g; Cholesterol: 264mg; Sodium: 388mg; Carbohydrates: 1.6g; Dietary Fiber: 0.5g; Protein: 8.3g

EGGS WITH FIVE FLAVORED SALTS

I have a few friends who keep a ready supply of boiled eggs in their fridge for when they want a breakfast or snack that is rich in protein (not to mention vitamins A and D, iron and choline). Great idea, but I just can't eat a plain ol' egg: for me, they need a little more pep. These flavored salts are easy to make and store. Of course, they can be used for a variety of foods, not just eggs.

An extra-large egg is 83 calories. Add a ¼ teaspoon of any of these salts and you are well under the 100-calorie limit. For all of them, place the ingredients in a small lidded glass container and mix well. Cover and store at room temperature for 6 months.

NUTMEG SALT
½ cup ground nutmeg
½ cup kosher salt

GINGER SALT
½ cup ground ginger
½ cup kosher salt

CURRY SALT
¼ cup curry powder
2 tablespoons ground cumin
½ cup kosher salt

FIVE-SPICE SALT
2 tablespoons Chinese
 five-spice powder
½ cup kosher salt

CUMIN SALT
2 tablespoons cumin
½ cup kosher salt

NUTRITION FACTS (per ¼ teaspoon salt): ■ NUTMEG SALT: Calories: 1; Calories from Fat: 1; Fat: 0.1g; Saturated Fat: 0mg; Cholesterol: 0mg; Sodium: 289mg; Carbohydrates: 0.1g; Dietary Fiber: 0g; Protein: 0.1g ■ GINGER SALT: Calories: 1; Calories from Fat: 0; Fat: 0.1g; Saturated Fat: 0g; Cholesterol: 0mg; Sodium: 289mg; Carbohydrates: 0.6g; Dietary Fiber: 0g; Protein: 0.0g ■ CURRY SALT: Calories: 1; Calories from Fat: 0; Fat: 0.0g; Saturated Fat: 0g; Cholesterol: 0mg; Sodium: 337mg; Carbohydrates: 0.1g; Dietary Fiber: 0g; Protein: 0.0g ■ FIVE-SPICE SALT: Calories: 0; Calories from Fat: 0; Fat: 0.0g; Saturated Fat: 0g; Cholesterol: 0mg; Sodium: 427mg; Carbohydrates: 0.2g; Dietary Fiber: 0g; Protein: 0.0g ■ CUMIN SALT: Calories: 0; Calories from Fat: 0; Fat: 0g; Saturated Fat: 0g; Cholesterol:0mg; Sodium: 472mg; Carbohydrates: 0g; Dietary Fiber: 0g; Protein: 0

FRIED EGG IN A PORTOBELLO CAP
SERVES 1

This is a great way to extend an egg. Portobello mushrooms have almost no calories—26 in an average cap—and lots and lots of flavor. If you become a fan, you can pre-roast several mushrooms at a time and store them, ready to go when needed!

1 portobello mushroom cap
1 large egg
½ teaspoon dried marjoram or oregano
¼ teaspoon kosher salt
Pinch black pepper
1 tablespoon chopped fresh Italian flat-leaf parsley leaves

■ Preheat the oven to 425°F. Place the mushroom, cap side up, on a baking sheet and roast 20 minutes. Transfer to a plate.
■ Place a nonstick skillet over medium heat and when it is hot, gently crack the egg into pan. Cook until the white starts to solidify into a creamy white color and the yolk thickens but doesn't harden. Gently flip the egg and cook about 1 minute on the other side. Transfer the egg to the mushroom, sprinkle with the marjoram, salt and pepper and then with the parsley.

NUTRITION FACTS: Calories: 100; Calories from Fat: 47; Fat: 5.2g; Saturated Fat: 1.6g; Cholesterol: 212mg; Sodium: 660mg; Carbohydrates: 6g; Dietary Fiber: 1.8g; Protein: 9g

DEVILED EGGS WITH CAPERS, ANCHOVIES AND OLIVES
SERVES 4

So called because of the traditional inclusion of hot spices, nowadays almost anything tasty is considered fair game in deviled eggs. Capers, olives and anchovies are a classic Italian trio that works really well here. If you want to make these eggs truly devilish, just add a little bit of crushed red pepper flakes.

4 large eggs
2 tablespoons low-fat Greek yogurt
1 tablespoon drained capers
1 teaspoon olive paste
1 anchovy fillet, chopped
1 tablespoon chopped fresh Italian
  flat-leaf parsley leaves, plus additional
  for garnish (optional)

■ Place the eggs in a saucepan, cover with cold water, and bring to a boil over high heat. Reduce the heat and continue boiling for 15 minutes. Transfer to a bowl of very cold water.
■ When the eggs are cool enough to handle, peel them under cold running water (this makes it easier to get the peel off without damaging the egg). Cut in half lengthwise. Remove the yolks and place them in a small mixing bowl. Add the yogurt, capers, olive paste, anchovy fillet and parsley and mash together.
■ Refill each egg half with the yolk mixture and sprinkle with the additional parsley, if desired.

NUTRITION FACTS: Calories: 84; Calories from Fat: 50; Fat: 5.7g; Saturated Fat: 1.7g; Cholesterol: 212mg; Sodium: 211mg; Carbohydrates: 1.1g; Dietary Fiber: 0g; Protein: 7.3g

CURRIED EGGS

SERVES 4

I find the flavor of curry powder irresistible and honestly feel there are few foods that don't benefit from its addition. Curry leaves, which are tangerine-like in fragrance and rarely found outside of India, are not related. Curry powder, a mixture of cumin, coriander, black pepper, chiles, fenugreek, ginger, cinnamon, cloves, cardamom and salt, was invented by the British to mimic the flavor of Indian foods. Make these slightly spicy, slightly sweet eggs four at a time so you can have some on hand at home or at work.

4 large eggs
2 tablespoons nonfat Greek yogurt
½ teaspoon curry powder (either spicy or sweet, depending on your taste)
1 tablespoon mango chutney
1½ teaspoons finely chopped fresh chives, plus additional for garnish (optional)
1 tablespoon chopped fresh cilantro leaves plus additional for garnish (optional)
¼ teaspoon black pepper

■ Place the eggs in a saucepan, cover with cold water and bring to a boil over high heat. Reduce the heat and continue boiling for 15 minutes. Transfer to a bowl of very cold water.

■ When the eggs are cool enough to handle, peel them under cold running water (this makes it easier to get the peel off without damaging the egg). Cut the eggs in half lengthwise. Remove the yolks and place them in a small mixing bowl. Add the yogurt, curry, chutney, chives, cilantro and black pepper and mash together.

■ Refill each egg half with the yolk mixture and sprinkle with the additional chives and cilantro, if desired.

NUTRITION FACTS: Calories: 84; Calories from Fat: 46; Fat: 5.2g; Saturated Fat: 1.7g; Cholesterol: 212mg; Sodium: 81mg; Carbohydrates: 2.7g; Dietary Fiber: 0g; Protein: 7g

EGG "SANDWICH"

SERVES 1

Originally produced in Genoa, Italy, Genoa salami is a variety of salami traditionally made from pork. Like other types of salami it is first cured, then left to ferment, and finally air-dried. Genoa salami pairs perfectly with eggs: it is considered to have a mild flavor but is actually quite rich.

1 romaine leaf
1 teaspoon Dijon mustard
1 large hardboiled egg, sliced
1 slice Genoa salami (.2 ounces)

▩ Place a romaine leaf on a clean surface and paint with the mustard. Add the egg slices and top with the salami. Roll and enjoy!

NUTRITION FACTS: Calories: 101; Calories from Fat: 68; Fat: 7.6g; Saturated Fat: 2.5g; Cholesterol: 195mg; Sodium: 283mg; Carbohydrates: 0.7g; Dietary Fiber: 0g; Protein: 7.6g

SALTY

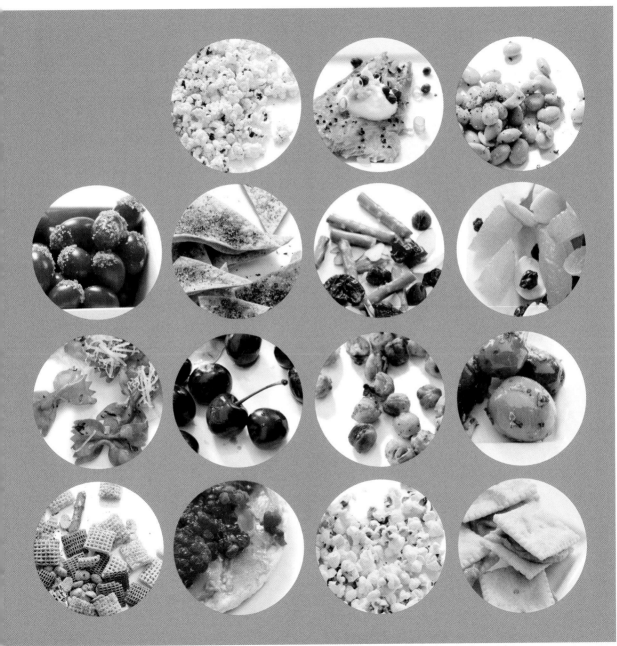

SPICED POPCORN
SERVES 2

Never mind the calorie load from movie popcorn, I hate the way I feel after eating all that fake butter. This popcorn is high in flavor, low in fat, and irresistible, for movie viewing or not.

5 cups air popped popcorn
1 teaspoon canola oil
½ teaspoon chipotle chili powder
2 teaspoons kosher salt
½ teaspoon ground cumin

■ Pour the popcorn into a large bowl, gently drizzle with the oil, add the chili powder, salt and cumin and toss well. Eat immediately.

NUTRITION FACTS: Calories: 99; Calories from Fat: 29; Fat: 3.3g; Saturated Fat: 0g; Cholesterol: 0mg; Sodium: 2328mg; Carbohydrates: 15.8g; Dietary Fiber: 3g; Protein: 2.7g

HOT AND SPICY PEANUTS

SERVES 18, ABOUT 1 TABLESPOON PLUS 2 TEASPOONS PER SERVING

This recipe makes a large quantity of nuts, but as long as you have willpower, you'll like having a ready supply in your fridge or freezer for unexpected company or occasions when you're in the mood for a peanut with a real kick. The heat of the spices will stop most people from eating too many.

1⅞ cups raw peanuts, skin on or off, depending on what you like
2 teaspoons canola oil
1 teaspoon kosher salt
½ teaspoon cayenne
½ teaspoon crushed red pepper flakes
½ teaspoon Hungarian paprika
½ teaspoon chipotle chili powder
¼ teaspoon chili powder

▨ Preheat the oven to 350°F. Place the nuts on a baking sheet; transfer to the oven and bake until lightly toasted, about 15 minutes. Transfer to a large bowl.
▨ Add the remaining ingredients, mix well and set aside until cooled, for at least 30 minutes and up to 2 hours. Transfer to a lidded jar and refrigerate.

NUTRITION FACTS: Calories: 97; Calories from Fat: 77; Fat: 8.5g; Saturated Fat: 1.2g; Cholesterol: 0mg; Sodium: 133mg; Carbohydrates: 2.7g; Dietary Fiber: 1.4g; Protein: 4.2g

STUFFED DATES
SERVES 1

The combination of sweet, salty, hard and chewy is absolutely amazing. At a surprisingly low 23 calories each, dates are rich and luscious; the addition of the blue cheese, nuts and prosciutto makes them absolutely decadent in flavor. It's hard to believe they are not totally decadent in calories as well.

3 dates, stone removed
1½ teaspoons blue cheese
3 pecan halves, lightly toasted or spiced

■ Cut open the dates and fill each cavity with ½ teaspoon blue cheese and a pecan half and then re-form into original shape. Serve immediately or cover and refrigerate up to overnight. Allow to come to room temperature before serving.

NUTRITION FACTS: Calories: 101; Calories from Fat: 26; Fat: 2.9g; Saturated Fat: 0.9g; Cholesterol: 3mg; Sodium: 59mg; Carbohydrates: 19.1g; Dietary Fiber: 2.2g; Protein: 1.7g

SMOKED TROUT ON FINN CRISP CRACKERS

SERVES 1

Although I love smoked salmon, smoked trout, which is flakier and less oily, is my newfound love. If you want to add heat, drizzle on a little Tabasco.

2 teaspoons whipped cream cheese
1 Finn Crisp cracker
1 ounce smoked trout
Freshly grated lemon zest

■ Spread the cream cheese on the Finn Crisp. Top with the trout and sprinkle with the lemon zest.

NUTRITION FACTS: Calories: 83; Calories from Fat: 25.5; Fat: 2.75; Saturated Fat: 0.5g; Cholesterol: 22mg; Sodium: 122mg; Carbohydrates: 5.6g; Dietary Fiber: 0g; Protein: 10.4

SMOKED TROUT WITH HORSERADISH

SERVES 1

A fter I work out, I seem to crave protein, and this is an easy and flavorful way to get it.

1¾ ounces smoked trout
1½ teaspoons Greek yogurt
½ teaspoon prepared horseradish
¼ teaspoon drained capers
1 small scallion, finely chopped

■ Place the trout on a plate, top with the yogurt, then the horseradish and then the capers. Serve garnished with the scallion.

NUTRITION FACTS: Calories: 100; Calories from Fat: 39; Fat: 4.3g; Saturated Fat: 0.8g; Cholesterol: 37mg; Sodium: 68mg; Carbohydrates: 0.9g; Dietary Fiber: 0g; Protein: 13.7g

DID YOU KNOW?

NUT SERVINGS EQUAL TO 100 CALORIES

7 whole almonds
3½ Brazil nuts
11 cashews
11 hazelnuts
5 macadamia nuts
16 peanuts
5 whole pecans
25 pistachios
4 whole walnuts

EDAMAME WITH WASABI
SERVES 4

High in protein, potassium and fiber, sweet and nutty in flavor, edamame—young soybeans—are an easy and nutritious snack. Luckily, edamame are readily available at most supermarkets these days, so you don't have to save your cravings for when you dine at Japanese restaurants.

1 cup edamame
¾ teaspoon wasabi powder
¼ teaspoon ground ginger
¾ teaspoon kosher salt

▪ Preheat the oven to 375°F. Line a baking sheet with parchment paper.
▪ Place everything in a bowl and toss well. Spill onto the prepared baking sheet in a single layer, and transfer to the oven. Roast until the beans begin to color, about 15 minutes. Serve warm or cold.

NUTRITION FACTS: Calories: 96; Calories from Fat: 39; Fat: 4.4g; Saturated Fat: 0.5g; Cholesterol: 0mg; Sodium: 446mg; Carbohydrates: 7.3g; Dietary Fiber: 2.8g; Protein: 8.3g

BLACK AND WHITE EDAMAME
SERVES 4

A lthough these are simple, the lavish use of salt and pepper makes them impossible to stop eating.

1 cup edamame, boiled
1 teaspoon kosher salt
1 teaspoon black pepper

Place the edamame, salt and pepper in a small bowl and toss well. Serve warm or chilled.

NUTRITION FACTS: Calories: 95; Calories from Fat: 39; Fat: 4.4g; Saturated Fat: 0.5g; Cholesterol: 0mg; Sodium: 591mg; Carbohydrates: 7.4g; Dietary Fiber: 2.8g; Protein: 8.3g

OREGANO-ROASTED FAVA BEANS

SERVES 4

Although fava beans—also known as broad beans, Windsor beans, English beans, horse beans, pigeon beans and field beans—take a lot of work to get out of their pods, it's well worth the time and fuss. Fava beans are most often used in Mediterranean cuisines fried or steamed, but I prefer them roasted.

Most herbs and spices pair well with fava beans but I especially like how the strong, almost pungent flavor of oregano contrasts with their slightly bitter, buttery, nutty taste. Favas are high in fiber, iron and protein, and very low in sodium and fat.

¾ **cup shelled fava beans (start with ¾ pound)**
½ **teaspoon olive oil**
½ **teaspoon dried Greek oregano**

■ Preheat the oven to 300°F. Line a baking sheet with a silicone mat or with parchment paper.
■ Place all the ingredients in a small bowl, toss well and spill onto the baking sheet. Bake until they are just starting to color and are dried out, about 5 minutes. Set aside to cool.

NUTRITION FACTS: Calories: 101; Calories from Fat: 9; Fat: 1g; Saturated Fat: 0g; Cholesterol: 0mg; Sodium: 4mg; Carbohydrates: 16.5g; Dietary Fiber: 7.1g; Protein: 7.4g

MARGERY'S TOMATOES
SERVES 2

My friend Margery Rubin swears by these vodka-drenched, curry-and-salt-dipped tomatoes. "You have to convince your guests to try these," she says, "but when they do, they're hooked." I can readily attest to that.

2½ cups grape or cherry tomatoes
1 tablespoon vodka or water
½ teaspoon kosher salt
¼ teaspoon curry powder

■ Place the tomatoes in a small bowl and each of the remaining ingredients in separate bowls. Dip the tomatoes in the vodka, then the salt, and then the curry powder. Eat!

NUTRITION FACTS: Calories: 94; Calories from Fat: 4; Fat: 0.4g; Saturated Fat: 0g; Cholesterol: 0mg; Sodium: 584mg; Carbohydrates: 19.9g; Dietary Fiber: 1.1g; Protein: 0.8g

TORTILLA CHIPS
SERVES 4

Unlike store-bought tortilla chips, home-baked chips are not loaded with fat or salt. However, be forewarned: they are just as hard to resist. I like to use scissors for cutting: it's much easier than using a knife!

3 tortillas, cut into triangles
1½ teaspoons olive oil
¾ teaspoon dried oregano
¾ teaspoon chili powder
¾ teaspoon kosher salt

■ Preheat the oven to 325°F. Line a baking sheet with parchment paper.
■ Place all the ingredients in a bowl and toss gently until the oil has coated most of the surfaces. Pile onto the baking sheet and cook until just beginning to color, about 10 minutes. Set aside to cool.

NUTRITION FACTS: Calories: 106; Calories from Fat: 29; Fat: 3.2g; Saturated Fat: 0g; Cholesterol: 0mg; Sodium: 554mg; Carbohydrates: 15.1g; Dietary Fiber: 1.6g; Protein: 2.8g

TOMATO SALSA

SERVES 2, ABOUT ½ CUP SALSA PER SERVING PLUS 3 TRIANGLES PITA BREAD

S alsa is so easy, so versatile and so delicious I don't really understand why anyone would buy it.

1½ pounds ripe beefsteak tomatoes, seeded, if desired, and finely diced
1 small red onion, finely chopped
2 garlic cloves, minced
1 bell pepper of any color, chopped
1 jalapeño or chipotle chile, seeded, if desired, and finely chopped (optional)
¼ cup finely chopped fresh cilantro leaves
¼ teaspoon cayenne pepper (optional)
¼ teaspoon kosher salt
1 tablespoon fresh lime juice
¾ pita bread, lightly toasted, cut into 6 triangles

Combine all the ingredients except for the pita bread, cover and refrigerate for at least 2 hours and up to overnight. Serve with pita bread triangles.

NUTRITION FACTS: Calories: 90; Calories from Fat: 5; Fat: 0.5g; Saturated Fat: 0g; Cholesterol: 0mg; Sodium: 199mg; Carbohydrates: 18.6g; Dietary Fiber: 2.2g; Protein: 3.2g

BUGS ON A LOG
SERVES 1

A peanut butter treat that doesn't—can't—stick to the roof of your mouth! Although the name is certainly kid friendly, this treat is most definitely not just for kids.

Although peanuts and peanut butter get a bad rap for being high in calories (and they are), they are also considered heart healthy (in reasonable quantities). Be sure to buy peanut butter with no added sugar: the best peanut butter is the kind you grind yourself. You don't need to rush out and buy a grinder: most natural food stores have grinders in their produce or bulk sections.

1 celery stick
1 tablespoon peanut butter
6 Craisins (dried cranberries)

■ Place the celery stick on a flat surface and fill with the peanut butter. Dot with the Craisins and eat!

NUTRITION FACTS: Calories: 103; Calories from Fat: 73; Fat: 8.1g; Saturated Fat: 1.7g; Cholesterol: 0mg; Sodium: 74mg; Carbohydrates: 6.6g; Dietary Fiber: 1.3g; Protein: 4g

GORP #1

SERVES 8, 2 TABLESPOONS PLUS 2 TEASPOONS PER SERVING

ore has it that GORP stands for "good old raisins and peanuts." Gorp, generally a crunchy, salty, chewy, sweet treat, can include a huge range of flavors and textures, as long as the sweet and salty are kept in balance. Make these in quantity to keep stashed in your car, purse, briefcase, kid's lunchbox and backpack.

⅓ cup Marcona almonds
¼ cup Craisins (dried cranberries)
⅓ cup semisweet chocolate chips
40 pretzel thins, broken

■ Place everything in a small bowl and toss. Divide into 8 little bags.

GORP #2

SERVES 8, ABOUT 3 TABLESPOONS PER SERVING

½ cup lightly toasted almonds
½ cup semisweet chocolate chips
½ cup dried apricots, chopped

■ Place everything in a small bowl and toss. Divide into 8 little bags.

NUTRITION FACTS: ■ GORP #1: Calories: 101; Calories from Fat: 42; Fat: 4.7g; Saturated Fat: 1.2g; Cholesterol: 0mg; Sodium: 77mg; Carbohydrates: 13.5g; Dietary Fiber: 1.6g; Protein: 2.2g ■ GORP #2: Calories: 104; Calories from Fat: 58; Fat: 6.4g; Saturated Fat: 1.7g; Cholesterol: 0mg; Sodium: 7mg; Carbohydrates: 10.2g; Dietary Fiber: 1.9g; Protein: 2.4g

GORP #3

SERVES 8, ABOUT 3 TABLESPOONS PER SERVING

⅓ cup white chocolate chips
½ cup plus 1 tablespoon Craisins (dried cranberries)
50 pretzel thins, just under 1 cup when broken

■ Place everything in a small bowl and toss. Divide into 8 little bags.

GORP #4

SERVES 8, ABOUT 2 TABLESPOONS PLUS 2 TEASPOONS PER SERVING

⅓ cup Marcona almonds or lightly toasted
    almonds
½ cup currants
½ cup dried apricots

■ Place everything in a small bowl and toss.
Divide into 8 little bags.

NUTRITION FACTS: ■ GORP #3: Calories:100; Calories from Fat: 23; Fat: 2.6g; Saturated Fat: 1.5g; Cholesterol: 1mg; Sodium: 103mg; Carbohydrates: 19.1g; Dietary Fiber: 1.2g; Protein: 1.2g ■ GORP #4: Calories: 94; Calories from Fat: 26; Fat: 3g; Saturated Fat: 0g; Cholesterol: 0mg; Sodium: 4mg; Carbohydrates: 17g; Dietary Fiber: 2g; Protein: 2g

GORP #5

SERVES 8, ¼ CUP PLUS 1½ TABLESPOONS PER SERVING

½ **cup raisins**
⅓ **cup lightly toasted peanuts**
2 **cups Corn Chex cereal**

■ Place everything in a small bowl and toss. Divide into 8 little bags.

GORP #6

SERVES 8, 1 TABLESPOON PLUS 2 TEASPOONS PER SERVING

½ **cup dried apricots, chopped**
⅓ **cup semisweet chocolate chips**
½ **cup Marcona or standard lightly toasted almonds**

■ Place everything in a small bowl and toss. Divide into 8 little bags.

NUTRITION FACTS: ■ GORP #5: Calories: 103; Calories from Fat: 33; Fat: 3.7g; Saturated Fat: 0g; Cholesterol: 0mg; Sodium: 102mg; Carbohydrates: 15.7g; Dietary Fiber: 1.2g; Protein: 2.7g ■ GORP #6: Calories: 95; Calories from Fat: 53; Fat: 5.9g; Saturated Fat: 1.4g; Cholesterol: 0mg; Sodium: 6mg; Carbohydrates: 9g; Dietary Fiber: 1.7g; Protein: 2.3g

GORP #7

SERVES 8, ABOUT ¼ CUP PER SERVING

¼ **cup raisins**
¼ **cup semisweet chocolate chips**
½ **cup lightly toasted almonds**
40 pretzel thins

■ Place everything in a small bowl and toss. Divide into 8 little bags.

GORP #8

SERVES 8, JUST OVER ¼ CUP PER SERVING

3 ounces small pretzel twists or sticks
⅓ **cup lightly toasted almonds**
½ **cup raisins**
1 ounce (⅔ cup) mini marshmallows

■ Place all the ingredients in a bowl and mix well. Store, covered, for up to 1 week.

NUTRITION FACTS: ■ GORP #7: Calories: 100; Calories from Fat: 46; Fat: 5.1g; Saturated Fat: 1g; Cholesterol: 0mg; Sodium: 76mg; Carbohydrates: 12.1g; Dietary Fiber: 1.5g; Protein: 2.5g ■ GORP #8: Calories: 101; Calories from Fat: 21; Fat: 2.3g; Saturated Fat: 0g; Cholesterol: 0mg; Sodium: 148mg; Carbohydrates: 19.3g; Dietary Fiber: 1.1g; Protein: 2.2g

PASTA CHIPS
SERVES 4

The original owners of Smartfood Popcorn made Pasta Chips in the 1980s. Called Zeus Chips, they were salty, cheesy, light and crunchy but not as firm as uncooked pasta. Very addictive! My recollection is that they were in existence barely a year. I have tried here to reproduce them, not an easy feat.

4 ounces medium shaped pasta, such as bowties or shells, cooked and cooled
1¼ teaspoons olive oil
½ teaspoon kosher salt
½ teaspoon dried basil
½ teaspoon dried oregano
1 tablespoon grated Parmesan cheese or powdered Cheddar cheese

■ Preheat the oven to 250°F. Line a baking sheet with parchment paper.
■ Place the pasta, oil, salt, basil and oregano in a bowl and toss well. Pour the pasta on the prepared baking sheet and transfer to the oven. Bake until very lightly browned and slightly crisp, 8 to 12 minutes. Sprinkle with the cheese.

NUTRITION FACTS: Calories: 100; Calories from Fat: 22; Fat: 2.4g; Saturated Fat: 0.5g; Cholesterol: 22mg; Sodium: 317mg; Carbohydrates: 15.7g; Dietary Fiber: 0g; Protein: 3.7g

PICKLED CHERRIES
SERVES 4

Pickled cherries are a French classic: vinegary, tart, just slightly sweet and salty, they are a delight to eat. Often deemed "super fruits" because of the high concentration of antioxidants, cherries have a large array of health benefits. Scientists suggest that having 1 to 2 servings (½ cup fresh, 1 cup frozen, or 1 cup juice) of cherries per day can reduce the risk of heart disease as well as help to prevent memory loss.

½ **cup white vinegar**
½ **cup water**
2 tablespoons sugar
½ **teaspoon kosher salt**
½ **pound cherries, rinsed, stems left on**
¼ **teaspoon whole black peppercorns**
1 bay leaf

▪ Place the vinegar, water, sugar and salt in a small saucepan and bring to a boil over high heat. Set aside.
▪ Prick each cherry with a needle, fork or skewer and transfer to a jar. Add the crushed peppercorns and bay leaf. Add the boiling liquid, being sure to cover the cherries completely.
▪ When the cherries have cooled, close the jar and set aside in a cold place for a few days before opening.

NUTRITION FACTS: Calories: 96; Calories from Fat: 0; Fat: 0g; Saturated Fat: 0g; Cholesterol: 0mg; Sodium: 303mg; Carbohydrates: 22.5g; Dietary Fiber: 0g; Protein: 0.2g

SPICY BLACK BEAN DIP
SERVES 18, ABOUT 1 TABLESPOON PER SERVING

A lthough they're high in calories, black beans serve as a good source of fiber. Serve this dip on endive, carrots, celery and jicama.

1 can (19 ounces) black turtle beans, drained and well rinsed
2 garlic cloves
¼ cup orange juice
½ teaspoon ground cumin
½ teaspoon kosher salt
Juice of ½ lime
2 tablespoons chopped fresh cilantro leaves
¼ to ½ teaspoon chipotle chili powder or cayenne pepper (optional)

▪ Place the beans and garlic in a food processor fitted with a steel blade and process until as smooth as possible, which is still a bit gritty. Add the orange juice, cumin, salt, lime juice, 1 tablespoon cilantro and chili powder, if desired.

▪ Transfer to a serving bowl, cover and refrigerate for at least 1 hour and up to 3 days or serve immediately garnished with the remaining 1 tablespoon cilantro.

NUTRITION FACTS: Calories: 104; Calories from Fat: 4; Fat: 0.4g; Saturated Fat: 0g; Cholesterol: 0mg; Sodium: 66mg; Carbohydrates: 19.2g; Dietary Fiber: 4.6g; Protein: 6.5g

TOASTED PEPITAS

SERVES 4, ABOUT 2 TABLESPOONS PER SERVING

Though most of us cook pumpkin seeds around Halloween after carving scary gremlins, pumpkin seeds are not just for kids: they are thought to be an aphrodisiac.

½ cup fresh pumpkin seeds
¾ teaspoon canola oil
½ teaspoon kosher salt

■ Preheat the oven to 350°F. Place the pumpkin seeds, oil and salt on a baking sheet and toss well. Transfer to the oven and bake until just lightly toasted, about 15 minutes. Set aside to cool.

NUTRITION FACTS: Calories: 101; Calories from Fat: 79; Fat: 8.8g; Saturated Fat: 1.6g; Cholesterol: 0mg; Sodium: 3mg; Carbohydrates: 3.1g; Dietary Fiber: 0.7g; Protein: 4.2g

ROASTED CHICKPEAS

SERVES 16, ABOUT 2 TABLESPOONS PER SERVING

After roasting, these chickpeas resemble super-low-fat nuts. The combination of the chickpea and the cumin is wonderful but if you don't like cumin, feel free to omit it or substitute coriander, curry powder or rosemary.

1 can (15.5 ounces) chickpeas, drained, rinsed well
  and dried
1 teaspoon olive oil
2½ teaspoons kosher salt
1½ teaspoons black pepper
¾ teaspoon ground cumin

■ Preheat the oven to 500°F. Place all the ingredients in a large bowl and toss well. Pour the mixture onto a baking sheet, transfer to the oven, and roast, shaking occasionally, until the chickpeas are firm and lightly browned, about 25 minutes. Set aside to cool.

NUTRITION FACTS: Calories: 103; Calories from Fat: 18; Fat: 2g; Saturated Fat: 0g; Cholesterol: 0mg; Sodium: 370mg; Carbohydrates: 16.8g; Dietary Fiber: 4.8g; Protein: 5.3g

ROASTED CITRUS OLIVES

SERVES 4

Though olives are shunned for their high fat content, they are quite low in calories, so the fact that a lot of their calories come from fat doesn't matter here. Just don't eat too many of these aromatic treats. If you don't feel like turning the oven on, these are also great uncooked.

2¼ cups assorted olives, such as Alphonso, Kalamata, Niçoise, Picholine and Sicilian Green
2 garlic cloves, minced
½ teaspoon dried Greek oregano
¼ teaspoon crushed red pepper flakes
½ teaspoon fennel seed
½ teaspoon kosher salt
½ teaspoon black pepper
½ teaspoon olive oil
Freshly grated zest of 1 orange
2 teaspoons chopped fresh rosemary
1 tablespoon chopped fresh Italian flat-leaf parsley leaves

■ Preheat the oven to 450°F. Place the olives, garlic, oregano, crushed red pepper, fennel, salt and pepper on a baking sheet and toss well. Transfer to the oven and roast until the olives are softened and sizzling hot, about 15 minutes. Turn off the heat, add the remaining ingredients, and serve immediately or at room temperature.

NUTRITION FACTS: Calories: 99; Calories from Fat: 79; Fat: 8.8g; Saturated Fat: 1.2g; Cholesterol: 0mg; Sodium: 951mg; Carbohydrates: 6.2g; Dietary Fiber: 3g; Protein: 0.9g

BABA GHANOUSH
SERVES 4, ABOUT ½ CUP PER SERVING

Originally from Syria and once considered esoteric, baba ghanoush has become so popular in the United States you can almost always find a huge variety in your neighborhood grocery store. However, you'll have an easier time controlling the fat if you make it yourself. Smoky, smooth and herby, baba ghanoush can be eaten on pita or, for even fewer calories, stuffed inside endive leaves. Eggplant is a nutrient-dense food that has almost no calories and no fat.

1 small eggplant, pricked with tines of a fork
1 to 2 garlic cloves
3 tablespoons tahini (sesame paste)
2 tablespoons fresh lemon juice
2 teaspoons freshly grated lemon zest
¼ cup finely chopped scallions
¼ cup finely chopped fresh cilantro leaves, plus additional for garnish
¼ cup finely chopped fresh mint leaves, plus additional for garnish
Kosher salt
Cayenne pepper (optional)
1 tablespoon pomegranate molasses

▧ Preheat the oven to 425°F. Place the eggplant in the oven and roast, turning occasionally, until it is very soft, about 45 minutes. Set aside to cool and when it is cool enough to handle, scoop out the flesh and transfer to a colander to drain. Press out and discard any liquid. Discard the skin.
▧ Place the eggplant, garlic and tahini in a food processor fitted with a steel blade and pulse until combined. Transfer to a bowl, add the remaining ingredients and mix well. Cover and refrigerate for at least 1 hour and up to overnight. Serve garnished with cilantro and mint leaves.

NUTRITION FACTS: Calories: 102; Calories from Fat: 56; Fat: 6.2g; Saturated Fat: 0.9g; Cholesterol: 0mg; Sodium: 19mg; Carbohydrates: 11.2g; Dietary Fiber: 3.7g; Protein: 2.9g

BBQ SNACK MIX
SERVES 13, JUST OVER ¼ CUP PER SERVING

2½ cups air-popped popcorn
1 cup mini pretzels
⅓ cup plus 1 tablespoon lightly roasted peanuts
1 teaspoon chili powder
¼ teaspoon onion powder
¼ teaspoon garlic powder
⅛ teaspoon dry mustard
1 teaspoon paprika
¼ teaspoon smoked salt
Canola oil spray

▓ Preheat the oven to 300°F. Line a baking sheet with parchment paper. Place the popcorn, pretzels and peanuts in a bowl and mix well. Add the remaining ingredients, except for the cooking spray, mix again, and place on the prepared baking sheet. Spray with canola oil for half a second, transfer to the oven, and bake until everything is well heated and just beginning to scent the kitchen, 7 to 10 minutes. Set aside to cool.

NUTRITION FACTS: Calories: 99; Calories from Fat: 48; Fat: 5.3g; Saturated Fat: 0.7g; Cholesterol: 0mg; Sodium: 103mg; Carbohydrates: 10.4g; Dietary Fiber: 1.8g; Protein: 3.8g

CAJUN CHEX MIX
SERVES 4, ABOUT ½ CUP PLUS 1 TABLESPOON PER SERVING

Chex mix, all grown up with classic Cajun seasonings.

½ **teaspoon dried Greek oregano**
½ **teaspoon garlic powder**
½ **teaspoon dried thyme**
¼ **teaspoon Hungarian paprika**
¼ **teaspoon kosher salt**
¼ **teaspoon cayenne**
¼ **teaspoon black pepper**
¾ **cup Corn Chex**
¾ **cup Rice Chex**
½ **cup Wheat Chex**
10 **thin pretzel sticks, broken into 4 pieces**
¼ **cup soy nuts**
Canola oil spray

■ Preheat the oven to 250°F.

■ In a small bowl combine the oregano, garlic powder, thyme, paprika, salt, cayenne and pepper and mix well. Place the Chex cereals, pretzels and soy nuts in a large bowl and toss well. Spray with canola oil for half a second. Add the spice mixture and mix well.

■ Place on a baking sheet and transfer to the oven. Bake until lightly browned, about 15 minutes. Set aside to cool. Serve or transfer to a jar for up to 1 week.

NUTRITION FACTS: Calories: 100; Calories from Fat: 16; Fat: 1.8g; Saturated Fat: 0g; Cholesterol: 0mg; Sodium: 200mg; Carbohydrates: 16.5g; Dietary Fiber: 2.5g; Protein: 3.9g

PEANUT BUTTER AND "JELLY"

SERVES 1

nstead of adding calorie- and sugar-rich jelly to the peanut butter, I added fresh raspberries, a healthier, fresher and more raspberry alternative. Corn Thins are a bit like rice cakes in look and texture, but are made from popped corn and are thinner. They have 26 calories each.

1 Real Foods brand Corn Thin
2 teaspoons natural peanut butter (no additional oil or sugar)
6 fresh raspberries, smushed

Place the corn cake on a cutting board and using a knife, spread the peanut butter. Top with the raspberries.

NUTRITION FACTS: Calories: 91; Calories from Fat: 48; Fat: 5.8g; Saturated Fat: 1.1g; Cholesterol: 0mg; Sodium: 49mg; Carbohydrates: 7.3; Dietary Fiber: 1.8g; Protein: 2.7g

CANDIED JALAPEÑO PEPPERS

SERVES 3

A strange combination, you say. No, no, these fiery peppers are a sweet treat for chile lovers.

1¼ cups fresh jalapeño peppers, sliced
¼ cup sugar
¼ cup water

■ Place the jalapeño slices, sugar and water in a small saucepan and bring to a boil over high heat. Reduce the heat and cook until the jalapeños are cooked and the liquid has boiled down to a thick syrup, 15 to 20 minutes. Set aside to cool and then transfer to a thick glass container and refrigerate.

NUTRITION FACTS: Calories: 76; Calories from Fat: 2; Fat: 0.2g; Saturated Fat: 0g; Cholesterol: 0mg; Sodium: 0mg; Carbohydrates: 18.9g; Dietary Fiber: 1.1g; Protein: 0.5g

DID YOU KNOW?

VEGETABLE SERVINGS EQUAL TO 100 CALORIES

16 cups arugula
2½ cups asparagus
⅔ avocado
1⅓ cups beets
3½ cups sliced bell peppers
2½ cups broccoli
1½ cup Brussels sprouts
4½ cups cabbage
4 medium carrots
3⅓ cups cauliflower
5 cups celery
16 stalks of celery
2 cucumbers
⅘ cup green peas
1 large head iceberg lettuce
3 cups cooked leeks
6⅔ cups sliced mushrooms
4 onions
100 radishes
4 cups raw rhubarb
14 cups spinach leaves
33 cherry tomatoes
10 plum tomatoes

POPCORN WITH BASIL AND PARMESAN

SERVES 1

M y childhood friend Lizzy Shaw gave me this recipe: it's too bad movie theaters aren't consulting her too.

2½ cups air popped popcorn
¼ teaspoon dried basil
¼ teaspoon kosher salt
¼ teaspoon crushed red pepper flakes (optional)
1 tablespoon Parmesan cheese

■ Preheat the oven to 300°F. Pour the popcorn into a large bowl and add the basil, salt and red pepper flakes, if desired. Toss well. Add the Parmesan and transfer to the oven for 5 minutes. Eat immediately.

NUTRITION FACTS: Calories: 100; Calories from Fat: 22; Fat: 2.4g; Saturated Fat: 1g; Cholesterol: 4mg; Sodium: 660mg; Carbohydrates: 16g; Dietary Fiber: 3g; Protein: 4.6g

HONEY PEANUT BUTTER BITES

SERVES 1

Most commonly known for its use in the child-favorite peanut butter and jelly sandwich, peanut butter is a staple in most American households. Made from a mixture of ground peanuts, natural sweeteners and salt, the FDA requires that peanut butter contain at least 90 percent peanuts. Although high in both calories and fat, peanuts contain a large amount of protein and are proven to help prevent breast cancer and adult diabetes.

1 teaspoon natural peanut butter (no additional oil or sugar)
½ teaspoon honey
8 Kashi Cheddar cheese crackers

■ Place the peanut butter and honey in a small bowl and mix well. Using a knife, place ¼ of the mixture on each of 4 crackers. Top with the remaining 4 crackers.

NUTRITION FACTS: Calories: 104; Calories from Fat: 51; Fat: 5.7g; Saturated Fat: 1g; Cholesterol: 0mg; Sodium: 103mg; Carbohydrates: 11.2g; Dietary Fiber: 0.5g; Protein: 2.6g

ROASTED RED PEPPER SPREAD

SERVES 4, ABOUT ¼ CUP PER SERVING

Since bell peppers are missing the capsaicin that makes hot peppers hot, this dip is more sweet than spicy. Use this spread to rev up an egg or on a rice cake (in which case use about 2 tablespoons).

2 large roasted red peppers, cut in large chunks
1 garlic clove
2 tablespoons fresh lemon juice
2 tablespoons farmer cheese
2 tablespoons olive oil
½ teaspoon kosher salt
¼ to ½ teaspoon cayenne or chipotle chili powder, or more to taste (optional)
¼ teaspoon black pepper
1 tablespoon chopped fresh Italian flat-leaf parsley leaves
1 tablespoon chopped fresh dill leaves (optional)

▨ Place the red peppers and garlic in a food processor fitted with a steel blade and pulse until well chopped but not minced. While the machine is running, add the lemon juice, cheese, oil, salt, cayenne, if desired, and pepper and process until smooth and thick.
▨ Transfer to a serving bowl. Cover and refrigerate for at least 1 hour. Serve garnished with the parsley and dill, if desired.

NUTRITION FACTS: Calories: 101; Calories from Fat: 69; Fat: 7.7g; Saturated Fat: 1.3g; Cholesterol: 3mg; Sodium: 325mg; Carbohydrates: 6g; Dietary Fiber: 1.8g; Protein: 2.2g

CREAMY AND CHEESY

CHEESE TORTILLA
SERVES 2

I like to make this cheesy, warm tortilla in a pan, because I like the crunchiness that "frying" creates. My children, on the other hand, like to make these in the microwave. Feel free to add other spices, herbs or vegetables.

1 tortilla
3 tablespoons part-skim mozzarella cheese
3 to 4 fresh tomato slices
1 tablespoon chopped fresh basil leaves

■ Place a tortilla on a cutting board. Sprinkle one half with the cheese. Top with the tomato slices and basil. Fold over and press down.
■ Place a medium nonstick skillet over medium heat and add the tortilla. Cook until the cheese has melted and the tortilla is lightly browned, about 4 minutes. Cut in half and serve immediately.

NUTRITION FACTS: Calories: 100; Calories from Fat: 32; Fat: 3.5g; Saturated Fat: 1.3g; Cholesterol: 6mg; Sodium: 134mg; Carbohydrates: 11.3g; Dietary Fiber: 1.2g; Protein: 4.8g

CHEESE-STUFFED DATES

SERVES 1

C ream cheese softens the sweetness of super-rich dates, a grand indulgence when you crave something sweet but don't want straight sugar or high calories. Very high in fiber, potassium and vitamin A, dates contain a wealth of amino acids that help digest carbohydrates.

1 tablespoon cream cheese
Freshly grated zest of ¼ orange
3 Medjool dates, pitted

■ Place the cream cheese and orange zest in a small bowl and mix together. Divide into 3 portions and stuff inside each date. Eat or cover and refrigerate for up to 5 days.

NUTRITION FACTS: Calories: 105; Calories from Fat: 32; Fat: 3.6g; Saturated Fat: 2.2g; Cholesterol: 11mg; Sodium: 30mg; Carbohydrates: 18.9g; Dietary Fiber: 2g; Protein: 1.4g

HORSERADISH YOGURT DIP

SERVES 1

R elated to wasabi and mustard, horseradish gives this yogurt dip some bite. If you want even more bite, go wild and add as much as you like: a teaspoon of horseradish is only 2 calories!

¼ cup low-fat Greek yogurt
1 tablespoon horseradish
2 carrots

▪ Place the yogurt and horseradish in a small bowl and mix well. Cover and refrigerate for at least 1 hour and up to 2 days. Scoop up the dip with the carrots.

NUTRITION FACTS: Calories: 94; Calories from Fat: 14; Fat: 1.5g; Saturated Fat: 0.9g; Cholesterol: 3mg; Sodium: 150mg; Carbohydrates: 15.6g; Dietary Fiber: 3.9g; Protein: 6.1g

RICE CAKE WITH GOAT CHEESE AND OLIVE PASTE

SERVES 1

You have to be a bit careful with rice cakes: all are not created equal. An average rice cake has 35 to 40 calories whereas a brown rice cake has 70. And rice cakes flavored with cheese, chocolate and so on, are even higher in calories. Since rice cakes don't have a lot of flavor, the tendency is to eat a lot of them: here I have topped one with two ingredients so high in flavor, just one will satisfy.

1 rice cake
1 tablespoon goat cheese
2 teaspoons olive paste

■ Place a rice cake on a plate and spread with the goat cheese. Top with the olive paste and eat!

NUTRITION FACTS: Calories: 99; Calories from Fat: 39; Fat: 4.3g; Saturated Fat: 1.6g; Cholesterol: 9mg; Sodium: 288mg; Carbohydrates: 8.4g; Dietary Fiber: 0.9g; Protein: 5.3g

CHICKPEA MASH

SERVES 8, ABOUT 3 TABLESPOONS DIP PLUS 1 CARROT AND 1 CELERY STALK

Similar to humus but lower in fat and not quite as creamy, chickpea mash can be used the same way: as a dip or an accompaniment to vegetables.

1 can (15.5 ounces) chickpeas, drained and rinsed
2 garlic cloves
½ cup nonfat Greek yogurt
1 tablespoon fresh lime juice
½ teaspoon ground cinnamon
½ teaspoon ground cumin
1 teaspoon chili powder
1 teaspoon curry powder
⅛ teaspoon ginger powder
¼ teaspoon kosher salt
8 carrots, cut up
8 celery stalks, cut up

■ Place the chickpeas and garlic in a food processor and pulse to finely chop. Add the remaining ingredients and process until smooth. Cover and refrigerate for at least 1 hour and up to 2 days. Scoop up the mash with the carrots and celery.

NUTRITION FACTS: Calories: 90; Calories from Fat: 10; Fat: 1.1g; Saturated Fat: 0g; Cholesterol: 1mg; Sodium: 266mg; Carbohydrates: 16.5; Dietary Fiber: 3.6g; Protein: 4.3g

JARSLBERG AND CHUTNEY IN RED LEAF
SERVES 1

Chutney, a chunky jam-like combination of dried and fresh fruits, vegetables, vinegar, sugar and spices, is one of my favorite condiments. Here, the chutney is paired with the creamy, slightly bitter Jarslberg cheese to yield a great flavor and texture combination.

1 red lettuce leaf
1 teaspoon whole grain mustard
1 teaspoon mango chutney
1 ounce slice light Jarlsberg cheese

■ Lay the leaf on a flat surface and brush with the mustard and chutney. Add the cheese and roll up.

NUTRITION FACTS: Calories: 99; Calories from Fat: 48; Fat: 5.4g; Saturated Fat: 3.3g; Cholesterol: 17mg; Sodium: 93mg; Carbohydrates: 8.3g; Dietary Fiber: 0g; Protein: 5g

WASA CRACKERS WITH CREAM CHEESE AND RADISHES

SERVES 1

particularly like Wasa crackers because they are, as their package boasts, "a satisfying foundation for healthy snacking." Their gritty, rough texture is particularly appealing with creamy, tart cheese.

1 Wasa cracker (45 calories)
2 tablespoons whipped cream cheese
4 radishes, very thinly sliced

Lay the cracker on a flat surface and spread with the cream cheese. Top with the radishes.

NUTRITION FACTS: Calories: 76; Calories from Fat: 4; Fat: 0.4g; Saturated Fat: 0g; Cholesterol: 2mg; Sodium: 245mg; Carbohydrates: 12.3g; Dietary Fiber: 0g; Protein: 6.3g

PARMESAN FLATS

SERVES 2

Delicate, lacy and wonderfully craggy and wacky looking, these Parmesan "crackers" are just what I need when I crave cheese but don't want all the calories. They are best served alone, as most dips are too heavy for pairing.

9 tablespoons shredded Parmesan cheese
1 teaspoon dried thyme

■ Preheat the oven to 350°F. Line a baking sheet with parchment paper. Place tablespoons of Parmesan cheese on the prepared baking sheet. Sprinkle with the thyme. Transfer to the oven and bake until melted and lightly colored, about 6 minutes. Set aside to cool.

NUTRITION FACTS: Calories: 98; Calories from Fat: 58; Fat: 6.5g; Saturated Fat: 3.9g; Cholesterol: 20mg; Sodium: 344mg; Carbohydrates: 1.2g; Dietary Fiber: 0g; Protein: 8.7g

BUFFALO BLUE CHEESE BBQ RICE CRACKERS

SERVES 1

was recently in a grocery store and eyed these BBQ-flavored rice crackers. Hoping to duplicate the flavors of Buffalo's famous chicken wings, I topped them with blue cheese. It's not an exact replica, but it is reminiscent.

⅓ ounce blue cheese
6 mini BBQ rice cakes
1 teaspoon chopped scallion

Divide the blue cheese among the rice cakes and spread. Sprinkle with scallions.

NUTRITION FACTS: Calories: 102; Calories from Fat: 51; Fat: 5.7g; Saturated Fat: 3.6g; Cholesterol: 14mg; Sodium: 293mg; Carbohydrates: 7.9g; Dietary Fiber: 0g; Protein: 4.8g

CUCUMBER SANDWICHES

SERVES 1

A little messy for ladies who lunch, but just as delicate.

1 English cucumber, sliced
2 tablespoons crumbled farmer cheese
1 tablespoon finely chopped chives, cilantro, dill or mint leaves

■ Place half the cucumber slices on a flat surface. Dot or spread the cheese evenly among them. Sprinkle with the herbs and top with the remaining cucumber slices.

NUTRITION FACTS: Calories: 96; Calories from Fat: 26; Fat: 2.9g; Saturated Fat: 1.6g; Cholesterol: 10mg; Sodium: 126mg; Carbohydrates: 11.1g; Dietary Fiber: 1.6g; Protein: 7.1g

GREEK YOGURT, ROASTED RED PEPPER AND MINT DIP

SERVES 4, ABOUT ¼ CUP DIP PER SERVING PLUS 1 CELERY STALK AND 1 CARROT

Traditionally made from ewe's milk, Greek yogurt is typically strained and as a result is much thicker than most yogurt. Its distinctive taste is very rich and described by some as similar to sour cream. It's hard to believe this low-calorie dip is also nonfat. Serve these with endive spears, carrots and celery sticks.

2 small red bell peppers, sliced open and seeded
1½ cups (12 ounces) low-fat Greek yogurt
1 garlic clove, minced
3 tablespoons chopped fresh mint leaves
¼ to ½ teaspoon crushed red pepper flakes
¼ teaspoon black pepper
¼ teaspoon kosher salt
4 celery stalks, cut in thick julienne
4 carrots, cut in thick julienne

■ Preheat the broiler. Place the pepper directly under the broiler and blacken on all sides. Transfer to a heavy plastic or paper bag, seal and let sweat for 10 to 15 minutes. Remove the pepper from the bag and discard the burnt skin. Coarsely chop the pepper and transfer to a colander. Squeeze out as much liquid as possible.
■ Transfer to a mixing bowl and add the remaining ingredients except the celery and carrots. Cover and refrigerate for at least 1 hour and up to overnight. Scoop up the dip with the carrots and celery.

NUTRITION FACTS: Calories: 98; Calories from Fat: 18; Fat: 2g; Saturated Fat: 0g; Cholesterol: 0mg; Sodium: 232mg; Carbohydrates: 12.7g; Dietary Fiber: 3.1g; Protein: 8.5g

WASA CRACKER WITH FARMER CHEESE AND SUN-DRIED TOMATOES

SERVES 1

After eating too many sun-dried tomatoes in the 1980s, I thought I would forever shun them. I stopped using them for years and years until I discovered that they had improved. They are now more flavorful and have a softer texture that makes them easier to use. Now I like them, particularly paired with mild and milky farmer cheese.

- **1 tablespoon plus 1 teaspoon (¾ ounce) farmer cheese**
- **1 multi grain Wasa cracker**
- **1 tablespoon (½ ounce) ready-to-eat (not oil-packed) sun-dried tomatoes**
- **2 basil leaves, shredded**

■ Place the farmer cheese on the cracker and sprinkle with tomatoes and basil.

NUTRITION FACTS: Calories: 93; Calories from Fat: 16; Fat: 1.8g; Saturated Fat: 1.1g; Cholesterol: 7mg; Sodium: 187mg; Carbohydrates: 18g; Dietary Fiber: 0g; Protein: 7.6g

PORTOBELLO MUSHROOM WITH MOZZARELLA AND TOMATO
SERVES 1

The solid texture and rich flavor of the portobello mushroom make it a perfect substitute for dough in this pizza-like delicacy.

1 small portobello mushroom cap, black gills removed
2 thin tomato slices
2½ tablespoons shredded low-fat mozzarella cheese
Pinch dried oregano
Pinch dried basil
Pinch crushed red pepper flakes
Pinch kosher salt

■ Preheat the oven to 425°F. Place the portobello cap on a baking sheet, transfer to the oven, and roast for 10 minutes. Transfer the baking sheet to a heatproof surface. Top the cap with the tomatoes and cheese. Sprinkle with oregano, basil, red pepper flakes and salt. Return to the oven and roast until the cheese melts, about 5 minutes. Serve immediately.

NUTRITION FACTS: Calories: 103; Calories from Fat: 35; Fat: 3.9g; Saturated Fat: 2.3g; Cholesterol: 10mg; Sodium: 260mg; Carbohydrates: 10.6g; Dietary Fiber: 2.9g; Protein: 9.1g

SPICED GOAT CHEESE BALLS

SERVES 4, 2 BALLS PER SERVING

nstead of cutting off a chunk of Cheddar cheese I often eat these wonderfully flavorful goat cheese treats when I need to head off serious predinner snacking.

2½ ounces goat cheese
1½ ounces farmer cheese
1 tablespoon chopped fresh Italian flat-leaf parsley leaves
2 teaspoons dried basil
1 teaspoon dried oregano
½ teaspoon crushed red pepper flakes (optional)
¼ teaspoon kosher salt
¼ teaspoon coarsely cracked black pepper

Place the goat and farmer cheeses in a small bowl and mix to combine. Divide into 8 balls. Place the herbs, spices, salt and pepper on a small plate and mix well. Roll the balls of cheese in the herb mix and leave on the plate. Cover and refrigerate for at least 30 minutes and up to overnight.

NUTRITION FACTS: Calories: 100; Calories from Fat: 66; Fat: 7.3g; Saturated Fat: 4.9g; Cholesterol: 22mg; Sodium: 250mg; Carbohydrates: 0.8g; Dietary Fiber: 0g; Protein: 7.3g

SPICY HERB DIP
SERVES 4, ABOUT ¼ CUP PLUS 1 TABLESPOON DIP PLUS 4 ASPARAGUS AND 1 CARROT PER SERVING

Creamy and tart with just a little bit of zing, serve this dip with raw vegetables like asparagus, carrots, cauliflower and broccoli.

1¼ cups low-fat Greek yogurt
1 teaspoon minced fresh gingerroot
2 garlic cloves, minced
1 jalapeño pepper, seeded, if desired, and minced
½ teaspoon ground cumin
Juice and freshly grated zest of 1 lime
2 tablespoons chopped fresh cilantro leaves
2 tablespoons chopped fresh Italian flat-leaf parsley leaves
16 asparagus spears
4 carrots, cut in thick julienne

■ Place everything, except the asparagus and carrots, in a mixing bowl and gently combine. Cover and refrigerate for at least ½ hour and up to 4 hours. Scoop up the dip with the asparagus and carrots.

NUTRITION FACTS: Calories: 97; Calories from Fat: 16; Fat: 1.8g; Saturated Fat: 1.1g; Cholesterol: 4mg; Sodium: 69mg; Carbohydrates: 13.8g; Dietary Fiber: 4g; Protein: 9g

VEGETABLE COTTAGE CHEESE

SERVES 1

Most people add fruit to cottage cheese but the addition of the vegetables makes it a more substantial savory treat. You don't need to be wedded to this particular combination: feel free to add broccoli, asparagus or whatever vegetable appeals to you!

½ cup plus 1 tablespoon nonfat cottage cheese
1 tablespoon chopped English cucumber
1 tablespoon chopped tomato
1 tablespoon chopped carrot
1 tablespoon chopped chive
½ tablespoon chopped red onion
¼ teaspoon dried oregano
Kosher salt
Black pepper

■ Place everything in a mixing bowl and gently combine. Cover and refrigerate for at least ½ hour and up to 4 hours.

NUTRITION FACTS: Calories: 100; Calories from Fat: 1; Fat: 0.1g; Saturated Fat: 0g; Cholesterol: 6mg; Sodium: 588mg; Carbohydrates: 6.7g; Dietary Fiber: 0.7g; Protein: 17.3g

CHUTNEY-STUFFED JALAPEÑO PEPPERS
SERVES 1

S weet, creamy, tart and spicy, these peppers are delightful. Depending on the method of preparation, jalapeños have a wide variety of heat levels. Fueled by capsaicin, this heat is especially intense around the seeds of the chile. If you like a lot of heat, leave the seeds inside, but if not, be sure to get all of them out. Additionally, handling fresh jalapeños can often cause mild skin irritation: if you are sensitive, use gloves and, either way, be sure to thoroughly wash each pepper before handling it.

4 jalapeño peppers, halved and carefully seeded
4 teaspoons low-fat Greek yogurt
1 tablespoon mango chutney

■ Place the peppers on a flat surface, rounded side down. Place 1 teaspoon yogurt inside 4 of the halves and ½ teaspoon chutney inside the 4 remaining halves. Place the halves together. Serve immediately or cover and refrigerate up to overnight.

NUTRITION FACTS: Calories: 67; Calories from Fat: 13; Fat: 1.4g; Saturated Fat: 0.5g; Cholesterol: 1mg; Sodium: 1515mg; Carbohydrates: 12.3g; Dietary Fiber: 2.3g; Protein: 3.2g

YOGURT AND TOMATO DIP

SERVES 4, ABOUT ½ CUP DIP PLUS 3 PITA TRIANGLES PER SERVING

Chunky, refreshing and substantial, this is a cross between a salad and a dip.

1 tomato, seeded and finely chopped
½ English cucumber, finely chopped
1 garlic clove, minced
1 tablespoon fresh mint leaves
¾ cup low-fat Greek yogurt
1½ pita breads, cut into 12 triangles total

■ Place everything, except the pita triangles, in a small bowl and mix well. Cover and refrigerate for at least 1 hour and up to overnight. Scoop up the dip with the pita triangles.

NUTRITION FACTS: Calories: 100; Calories from Fat: 11; Fat: 1.2g; Saturated Fat: 0.7g; Cholesterol: 2mg; Sodium: 137mg; Carbohydrates: 16.6g; Dietary Fiber: 1g; Protein: 6.1g

HERB CHEESE

SERVES 2, ABOUT ½ CUP PER SERVING PLUS 3 CELERY STALKS

I was first introduced to this creamy, herby dip when I was in college and worked in a food shop called Essential Ingredients. I have lightened the original by substituting Greek yogurt, which I now prefer, for cream cheese and buttermilk.

7 ounces low-fat Greek yogurt
½ cup finely chopped fresh Italian flat-leaf parsley leaves
2 garlic cloves, minced
1 tablespoon finely chopped fresh basil leaves
1 tablespoon finely chopped fresh oregano
2 teaspoons finely chopped thyme leaves
¼ teaspoon black pepper
¼ teaspoon kosher salt
6 celery stalks, cut up

Place all the ingredients, except the celery, in a small bowl and combine well. Cover and refrigerate for at least 1 hour and up to 2 days. Scoop up the dip with the celery.

NUTRITION FACTS: Calories: 93; Calories from Fat: 23; Fat: 2.5g; Saturated Fat: 1.6g; Cholesterol: 5mg; Sodium: 374mg; Carbohydrates: 9.7g; Dietary Fiber: 2.8g; Protein: 9.8g

WATERMELON SANDWICH
SERVES 1

This is perhaps the wackiest recipe in the book, but don't turn the page. The first time I tried this refreshing treat, I kept making it over and over again. The contrast of the creamy, tart goat cheese with the sweet watery melon is remarkable.

Although high in sugar, watermelon also contains a high concentration of antioxidants, specifically those that help to protect against diabetes, colon cancer and arthritis. Additionally, watermelon contains lycopene, a carotenoid antioxidant. Most notably found in tomatoes, lycopene has been proven to lower the risk of breast and lung cancer.

$\frac{1}{16}$ **of a watermelon (about a 5 x 3-inch wedge), rind removed, sliced in two equal pieces**
1 ounce goat cheese
$\frac{1}{8}$ **teaspoon kosher salt**
$\frac{1}{8}$ **teaspoon anise or fennel seed (optional)**

■ Place 1 watermelon slice on a cutting board and top with the cheese. Top with the remaining slice. Sprinkle with salt and anise, if desired.

NUTRITION FACTS: Calories: 99; Calories from Fat: 42; Fat: 4.6g; Saturated Fat: 3.1g; Cholesterol: 13mg; Sodium: 190mg; Carbohydrates: 11.1g; Dietary Fiber: 0.6g; Protein: 4.7g

TZATZIKI

SERVES 6, ABOUT ⅓ CUP DIP PER PERSON

This classic Greek dip is mostly cucumber and mint, more chunky than smooth.

2 cups low-fat Greek yogurt
1 large English cucumber, quartered and thinly sliced
2 garlic cloves, minced
¼ cup finely chopped fresh mint leaves, plus additional
   for garnish
¼ to ½ teaspoon kosher salt
12 radishes
2 carrots, cut into thick julienne
2 toasted pita breads, cut into triangles

■ Place the yogurt, cucumber, garlic, mint and salt in a mixing bowl; mix well and transfer to a serving bowl. Cover and refrigerate for at least 1 hour and up to 2 days. Serve garnished with the additional mint. Scoop up the dip with the radishes, carrots and pita.

NUTRITION FACTS: Calories: 99; Calories from Fat: 18; Fat: 2g; Saturated Fat: 1.3g; Cholesterol: 4mg; Sodium: 176mg; Carbohydrates: 13.6g; Dietary Fiber: 6.5g; Protein: 9.3g

GREEN GODDESS DRESSING
SERVES 2

A little bit of this creamy, highly flavored and slightly biting dressing will suffice: I especially like it on iceberg and romaine lettuces with chunks of tomato. It's also great as a dip for endive leaves.

½ cup flat-leaf spinach leaves
¼ cup fresh Italian flat-leaf parsley leaves, plus additional for garnish
1 garlic clove, sliced
2 anchovy fillets
1 tablespoon capers
2 scallions, green and white parts included
2 sprigs fresh tarragon leaves
½ cup low-fat Greek yogurt
1 tablespoon mayonnaise
¼ teaspoon black pepper
½ head iceberg lettuce
1 tomato, diced

■ Place the spinach, parsley, garlic, anchovy fillets, capers, scallions and tarragon in a blender or food processor and process until smooth. Add the yogurt, mayonnaise and pepper and mix by hand to combine. Transfer to a serving bowl, cover, and refrigerate for up to 1 week or serve immediately, garnished with additional parsley leaves.
■ Place half of the lettuce and half of the diced tomatoes on 2 plates. Top each with half the dressing.

NUTRITION FACTS: Calories: 97; Calories from Fat: 37; Fat: 4.1g; Saturated Fat: 1.1g; Cholesterol: 7mg; Sodium: 364mg; Carbohydrates: 10.4g; Dietary Fiber: 2.6g; Protein: 6.9g

STUFFED HOLLOWED-OUT BAGEL

SERVES 1

Farmer cheese is a flavor cross between cream cheese, ricotta cheese and cottage cheese. It's actually cottage cheese with all the moisture drained out, so it's particularly great for any application where you want a drier consistency, such as for stuffing into a bagel.

½ **half plain bagel, inside doughy part scooped out**
1½ **tablespoons farmer cheese**

■ Place the scooped out bagel on a flat surface and fill with the farmer cheese. Eat!

NUTRITION FACTS: Calories: 104; Calories from Fat: 21; Fat: 2.3g; Saturated Fat: 1.2g; Cholesterol: 7mg; Sodium: 206mg; Carbohydrates: 13.1g; Dietary Fiber: 0.6g; Protein: 6.4g

PITA WITH YOGURT AND CUKES
SERVES 2

The calories in pita bread vary hugely so be sure to read the labels. The reduced carbohydrate breads are also lower in calories: my favorite is Joseph's Flax, Oat Bran & Whole Wheat Flour Pita Bread. In fact, I prefer its flavor and texture to all others.

1 reduced-carb pita bread, split
½ cup low-fat Greek yogurt
1 tablespoon plus 2 teaspoons feta cheese
1 cup thinly sliced English cucumbers
2 teaspoons chopped fresh mint leaves
Kosher salt
Black pepper

■ Place the pita halves on a flat surface. Place a layer of yogurt on the bottom, sprinkle with the feta cheese, and top with the cucumbers. Sprinkle with the mint leaves and add salt and pepper to taste. Serve immediately.

NUTRITION FACTS: Calories: 99; Calories from Fat: 27; Fat: 3g; Saturated Fat: 2.1g; Cholesterol: 10mg; Sodium: 249mg; Carbohydrates: 11.4g; Dietary Fiber: 0.7g; Protein: 7.4g

SPICY SESAME NORI COTTAGE CHEESE
SERVES 1 (BUT MAKES A BIG BATCH OF THE SPICE MIX FOR FUTURE USE)

Inspired by a recipe from pal chef Stan Frankenthaler, this mixture has a flavor that most people will have a hard time wrapping their brain around (as I did), but the unusual and mysterious combination will leave you smitten. To make it worth your time, make a big batch—about 1 1/4 cups—of the Spicy Sesame Nori Mix. However, for the sake of calorie counting, I am assuming 1 teaspoon spice mix per 1/2 cup cottage cheese.

Usually sold in dried rectangular sheets, nori is the Japanese name for edible seaweed and is most commonly found in sushi. It is green-black in color, has a very faint fishy flavor and is high in dietary fiber, protein and an array of vitamins.

TO MAKE A BIG BATCH OF SPICY SESAME NORI MIX:
3/4 cup sesame seeds, white or a combination of white and black
2 tablespoons coriander seeds
1/4 cup crushed red pepper flakes
2 tablespoons chipotle flakes (or additional
  crushed red pepper flakes if not available)
1 sheet nori, finely diced

TO SERVE:
1/4 cup cottage cheese
1 teaspoon Spicy Sesame Nori Mix

■ TO MAKE THE SPICE MIX: Place the sesame and coriander seeds in a small cast iron skillet and cook over medium heat, stirring to prevent burning, until fragrant, 2 to 3 minutes. Set aside to cool. Transfer to a lidded jar. Add the red pepper flakes, chipotle flakes and nori and mix well. Store at room temperature up to 1 month.

■ TO SERVE: Place the cottage cheese in a small bowl and sprinkle with 1 teaspoon spice mix.

NUTRITION FACTS (for ½ cup cottage cheese and 1 teaspoon spice mix): Calories: 93; Calories from Fat: 19; Fat: 2.2g; Saturated Fat: 0.7g; Cholesterol: 5mg; Sodium: 492mg; Carbohydrates: 3.8g; Dietary Fiber: 0g; Protein: 14.4g

WHIPPED GOAT CHEESE
SERVES 6, ABOUT ¼ CUP PER SERVING

Crunchy and juicy, endive is the perfect dipper for the creamy, tart goat cheese.

4 ounces goat cheese
½ cup buttermilk
¼ teaspoon chopped fresh basil leaves
2 tablespoons chopped sun-dried tomatoes
1 head endive, leaves separated

■ Place the goat cheese in a small mixing bowl and, using a fork, mash until creamy. Add a small amount of buttermilk and mash. Slowly and then more quickly, continue adding the buttermilk until the mixture is creamy and thick. Add the basil and tomatoes, mix well, cover, and refrigerate for at least 1 hour and up to 2 days. Scoop up the goat cheese with the endive leaves.

NUTRITION FACTS: Calories: 99; Calories from Fat: 67; Fat: 7.4g; Saturated Fat: 5.1g; Cholesterol: 22mg; Sodium: 93mg; Carbohydrates: 1.2g; Dietary Fiber: 0g; Protein: 6.7g

STRAWBERRY SANDWICH

SERVES 1

When I was in high school I specifically went to a now-defunct restaurant only to eat a version of this sandwich: its demise doesn't stop me from enjoying it still.

½ slice Mestemacher or other dense 3-grain bread (equal to 65 calories)
2 teaspoons farmer cheese
3 strawberries, sliced
½ teaspoon honey
Coarsely ground black pepper (optional)

■ Place the bread on a plate and spread with the farmer cheese. Top evenly with the strawberries and drizzle with the honey. Add black pepper, if desired. Cut in half and eat.

NUTRITION FACTS: Calories: 104; Calories from Fat: 18; Fat: 1.9g; Saturated Fat: 0.5g; Cholesterol: 3mg; Sodium: 236mg; Carbohydrates: 18.1g; Dietary Fiber: 3.7g; Protein: 3.9g

CRUNCHY

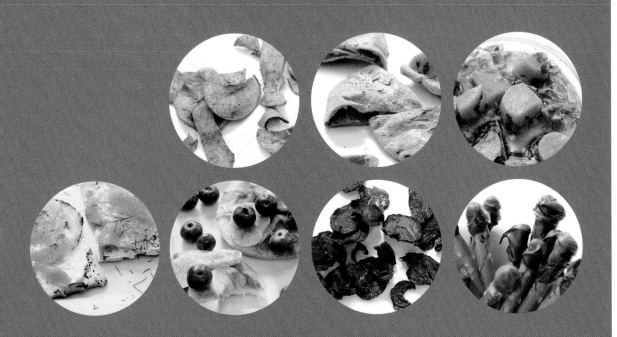

APPLE CHIPS

SERVES 4

These chips bear no relation to those you buy at the market: the intensity of their flavor is much deeper and more apple-y, and their texture is crispy rather than soft. To ensure crispness, slice the apples as thinly as possible: slice one side and then turn the apple ¼ of the way and slice smaller pieces (they won't be round) and keep going. The slices don't have to be uniform.

- **2 tablespoons sugar**
- **1 tablespoon ground cinnamon**
- **4 Granny Smith or other tart apples, thinly sliced**

▪ Preheat the oven to 250°F. Line 2 baking sheets with parchment paper.

▪ Place the sugar and cinnamon in a large bowl and mix well. Add the apple slices and toss until most of both sides of the apples are well coated (no need to get crazy if they aren't completely coated). Pour the apples, in a single layer, onto the baking sheets, transfer to the oven and bake until lightly browned and just crisp, about 2 hours. Set aside to cool and then transfer to a jar or plastic bag.

NUTRITION FACTS: Calories: 100; Calories from Fat: 2; Fat: 0.3g; Saturated Fat: 0g; Cholesterol: 0mg; Sodium: 2mg; Carbohydrates: 26.7g; Dietary Fiber: 4.2g; Protein: 0.4g

PITA TRIANGLES
SERVES 8, 8 TRIANGLES PER SERVING

Y ou can use just about any dried herb or spice for these crispy chips, but I especially like herbes de Provence, a mixture of savory, rosemary, cracked fennel, thyme, basil, tarragon, lavender and marjoram.

4 small whole wheat or reduced carb pita breads, cut into eighths
1 teaspoon olive oil
1 teaspoon herbes de Provence
¼ teaspoon kosher salt

■ Preheat the oven to 425°F. Lightly brush each pita eighth with oil and sprinkle with the herbes de Provence and salt. Place the triangles on a baking sheet. Transfer to the oven and cook until lightly golden, about 5 minutes. Eat immediately or set aside to cool.

NUTRITION FACTS: Calories: 103; Calories from Fat: 14; Fat: 1.6g; Saturated Fat: 0g; Cholesterol: 0mg; Sodium: 278mg; Carbohydrates: 20.1g; Dietary Fiber: 2.7g; Protein: 3.6g

PICKLED CARROTS WITH CARAWAY

SERVES 3

Pickling is the process of preserving foods by fermentation: using a solution of salt, various seasonings and water. When left to sit for at least a week, the carrot "pickles" and develops a slightly salty-sour taste.

1½ cups water
3 ounces unseasoned rice vinegar
¼ teaspoon caraway seed
1 tablespoon sugar
1 tablespoon kosher salt
½ teaspoon very coarsely crushed black peppercorns
1 pound trimmed carrots, cut into sticks
¼ cup finely chopped fresh Italian flat-leaf parsley leaves

■ Place the water, vinegar, caraway seed, sugar, salt and pepper in a nonreactive pot and bring to a boil. Cook until the sugar has dissolved, about 2 minutes. Add the carrots and parsley and set aside to cool to room temperature. Transfer to a container and refrigerate for at least 1 week and up to 1 month.

NUTRITION FACTS: Calories: 102; Calories from Fat: 4; Fat: 0.4g; Saturated Fat: 0g; Cholesterol: 0mg; Sodium: 2436mg; Carbohydrates: 19.3g; Dietary Fiber: 4.6g; Protein: 1.6g

SALMON AK-MAK

SERVES 1

The quintessential combination of smoked salmon and cream cheese on an Ak-Mak cracker instead of a bagel.

1 Ak-Mak cracker
1 tablespoon cream cheese
¾ ounce smoked salmon (1 slice)
1 very thin slice red onion
½ teaspoon chopped fresh dill
Pinch black pepper
¼ lemon

■ Place the Ak-Mak cracker on a flat surface and spread with the cream cheese. Top with the salmon and red onion. Sprinkle with dill and black pepper. Squeeze a bit of lemon juice on top.

NUTRITION FACTS: Calories: 85; Calories from Fat: 45; Fat: 4.6g; Saturated Fat: 2.4g; Cholesterol: 16mg; Sodium: 506mg; Carbohydrates: 6.4g; Dietary Fiber: 0g; Protein: 1.8g

PEANUT BUTTER–BANANA-APPLE BITES

SERVES 1

Certainly a snack most beloved by children, but most of the adults I know also love these little bites. The flavors and textures cover all the bases: crunchy, creamy, smooth, sweet and tart with a touch of cinnamon spiciness.

2 thin slices apple
2 teaspoons peanut butter
¼ banana, sliced
⅛ teaspoon sugar
⅛ teaspoon cinnamon
14 blueberries (optional)

■ Place the apple slices on a flat surface and spread with the peanut butter. Top with the banana. Sprinkle with the sugar, cinnamon and, if desired, the blueberries.

NUTRITION FACTS: Calories: 95; Calories from Fat: 49; Fat: 5.5g; Saturated Fat: 1.2g; Cholesterol: 0mg; Sodium: 60mg; Carbohydrates: 10.5g; Dietary Fiber: 1.7g; Protein: 3g

FAVA BEAN PUREE
SERVES 6, ABOUT 2 TABLESPOONS PER SERVING

Bright green and silky smooth, this humus-like recipe was inspired by Boston restaurateurs Lydia Shire and Susan Regis.

1 cup fresh fava beans, shelled
4 garlic cloves, chopped
2 teaspoons olive oil
1 tablespoon fresh lemon juice
½ teaspoon kosher salt
½ teaspoon black pepper
¼ cup chopped fresh basil leaves
2 thin slices lemon

■ Place a large bowl on the countertop and fill with ice. Bring a large pot of water to a boil over high heat. Add the beans to the boiling water and cook until they turn bright green, about 2 minutes. Transfer to the ice bath to cool; drain and set aside.

■ Place the beans and garlic in the bowl of a food processor fitted with a steel blade and puree. While the machine is running, gradually add the oil, lemon juice, salt and pepper. Transfer to a serving bowl and add the basil by hand. Cover and refrigerate for up to 2 days or serve immediately garnished with the lemon.

NUTRITION FACTS: Calories: 103; Calories from Fat: 17; Fat: 1.9g; Saturated Fat: 0g; Cholesterol: 0mg; Sodium: 198mg; Carbohydrates: 15.6g; Dietary Fiber: 6.4g; Protein: 6.7g

BEET CHIPS

SERVES 4

Beet chips are indescribably delicious. The cooking time will vary depending upon how thinly you are able to slice the beets, so keep an eye on the oven!

8 beets, boiled or roasted until soft, peeled and sliced as thinly as possible
1 teaspoon kosher salt
1 teaspoon olive oil

■ Preheat the oven to 400°F. Line 2 baking sheets with parchment paper.
■ Place the beets, salt and oil in a large bowl and toss until most of both sides of the beets are well coated. Pour the beets in a single layer onto the baking sheets, transfer to the oven, and bake until they are beginning to brown on the edges and are just crisp, about 40 minutes. Set aside to cool and then transfer to a jar or plastic bag for up to 3 days. If they become too moist, simply pop them in a 300°F oven for about 5 minutes.

NUTRITION FACTS: Calories: 98; Calories from Fat: 13; Fat: 1.5g; Saturated Fat: 0g; Cholesterol: 0mg; Sodium: 735mg; Carbohydrates: 19.9g; Dietary Fiber: 4g; Protein: 3.4g

CHOCOLATE MATCHSTICKS

SERVES 1

My childhood friend Cynthia Stuart introduced me to this quintessential salty-sweet combination many years ago, but I have to admit I consider this rendition pure genius! Just see how cool they look!

15 pretzel thins (about ½ ounce)
2 teaspoons semisweet chocolate morsels

▓ Place the chocolate morsels on a small plate and microwave for 10 seconds. Stir. Continue microwaving until the chocolate has melted, about 40 seconds. Take 1 pretzel stick and dip the end in the chocolate. Dip again. Continue with all the pretzels. If there is any chocolate remaining, keep dipping the pretzels until the chocolate has been used up and the tips are well coated. Serve immediately or set aside at room temperature for up to 4 hours.

NUTRITION FACTS: Calories: 100; Calories from Fat: 27; Fat: 3g; Saturated Fat: 1.7g; Cholesterol: 0mg; Sodium: 192mg; Carbohydrates: 17.2g; Dietary Fiber: 1.1g; Protein: 2.1g

CARBS

SCOTTISH OATMEAL SCONES

SERVES 16, 1 SCONE PER SERVING

I love scones and have been working on perfecting my recipe for years. Bakery and coffee shop scones have become so sugar laden and ingredient heavy (honestly, I just don't see how a chocolate chip belongs in a scone) they barely resemble their Scottish inspiration, which is soft, delicate, light and just flaky.

1 cup all purpose flour
¾ cup graham flour
¾ cup old fashioned oats
1 tablespoon sugar
¼ teaspoon kosher salt
¾ teaspoon baking soda
1 teaspoon baking powder
**6 tablespoons unsalted butter, frozen and sliced
     into 8 pieces**
⅔ cup skim milk buttermilk or yogurt

▓ Preheat the oven to 400°F. Line a baking sheet with parchment paper.
▓ Place the flours, oats, sugar, salt, baking soda and baking powder in a large bowl and mix well. Add the butter and cut in with 2 forks until the mixture resembles coarse cornmeal. Add the buttermilk and mix until just combined. Do not overmix.
▓ Transfer to a floured surface and knead 4 times. Pat into 2 circles and cut each circle into 8 small triangles. Transfer to the prepared baking sheet and bake until they are beginning to brown, 10 to 12 minutes. Serve warm or at room temperature.

NUTRITION FACTS: Calories: 100; Calories from Fat: 43; Fat: 4.8g; Saturated Fat: 2.8g; Cholesterol: 12mg; Sodium: 143mg; Carbohydrates: 12.8g; Dietary Fiber: 1g; Protein: 2g

MINI CRANBERRY MUFFINS
SERVES 12, 2 MUFFINS PER SERVING

These tiny, tart muffins are for cranberry lovers. You can substitute raspberries or blueberries if you wish. If you don't have mini muffin tins, you can make these in regular muffin tins, but then you can only eat half a muffin.

¾ cup all purpose flour
1 tablespoon wheat bran
1 tablespoon wheat germ
2 tablespoons cornmeal
2 tablespoons sugar
1 teaspoon baking powder
¼ teaspoon baking soda
¼ teaspoon kosher salt
1 cup fresh cranberries
4 tablespoons (½ stick) unsalted butter
1 large egg
½ cup plain low-fat yogurt
¼ teaspoon vanilla extract
½ teaspoon freshly grated orange zest

■ Preheat the oven to 375°F. Place mini liners in 2 mini muffin/cupcake tins (or use nonstick tins).
■ Place the flour, wheat bran, wheat germ, cornmeal, sugar, baking powder, baking soda and salt in a medium-size bowl. Add the cranberries and stir to combine. Place the remaining ingredients in a small bowl and mix well. Add to the flour mixture and stir until just combined; do not overmix.
■ Using a large spoon, place spoonfuls of the mix into the prepared tins. Transfer to the oven and bake until golden, about 15 minutes. Turn out of the pans and serve immediately or cool to room temperature. Store, covered, up to overnight or freeze for up to 1 month.

NUTRITION FACTS: Calories: 95; Calories from Fat: 42; Fat: 4.6g; Saturated Fat: 2.7g; Cholesterol: 28mg; Sodium: 116mg; Carbohydrates: 11.5g; Dietary Fiber: 0.9g; Protein: 2.3g

DID YOU KNOW?

POPULAR CANDY SERVINGS EQUAL TO 100 CALORIES

½ Kit Kat bar
⅔ cup mini marshmallows
29 M&M'S
10 Peanut M&M'S
⅓ Snickers bar
⅓ 3 Musketeers bar
½ York Peppermint patty

TABOULI

SERVES 8

When I started making tabouli, it seemed esoteric, but now it's standard American fare. I've been making tabouli for more years than I care to count, but I rarely make any changes to the recipe. It's just perfect the way it is!

¾ cup bulgur wheat
1 cup boiling water
3 beefsteak tomatoes, diced
1½ cups chopped fresh Italian flat-leaf parsley leaves
½ English cucumber, diced (about 1 cup)
⅓ cup chopped red onion
¼ cup chopped fresh mint leaves
2 tablespoons olive oil
2 tablespoons fresh lemon juice
2 garlic cloves, minced
½ teaspoon kosher salt

■ Place the bulgur and water in a bowl, cover, and let sit until the bulgur has softened, about 25 minutes.
■ In the meantime, place the remaining ingredients in a bowl and set aside. When the bulgur is tender and has cooled, add it to the bowl with the tomatoes, cover and refrigerate for at least 1 hour and up to overnight.

NUTRITION FACTS: Calories: 95; Calories from Fat: 34; Fat: 3.8g; Saturated Fat: 0.5g; Cholesterol: 0mg; Sodium: 159mg; Carbohydrates: 14.4g; Dietary Fiber: 3.7g; Protein: 2.7g

FARRO PANZANELLE
SERVES 4, ABOUT 1 CUP PER SERVING

I love farro—a slightly chewy, nutty ancient grain. Farro, also known as emmer wheat, is not always easy to find but well worth the search: when you find it, buy two bags. Panzanelle is an Italian bread salad, but here I have substituted the bread with farro.

½ cup farro
2 large or 3 beefsteak tomatoes, diced (about 2½ cups)
¾ cup diced English cucumber
¼ to ⅓ cup diced red onion (about ¼ medium)
¼ cup scallions, thinly sliced
2 tablespoons chopped fresh basil leaves
½ cup chopped fresh Italian flat-leaf parsley leaves
1 tablespoon extra-virgin olive oil
1½ teaspoons red wine vinegar
Kosher salt and black pepper

Fill a small saucepan with water and bring to a boil over high heat. Add the farro and cook until it is tender, 15 to 20 minutes. Drain. Transfer to a large mixing bowl and set aside to cool to room temperature. Add the tomatoes, farro, cucumbers, onion, scallions, basil and parsley and gently mix. Add the oil, vinegar, and salt and pepper to taste and gently mix again. Cover and refrigerate for at least 1 hour and up to overnight.

NUTRITION FACTS: Calories: 84; Calories from Fat: 34; Fat: 4g; Saturated Fat: 1g; Cholesterol: 0mg; Sodium: 13mg; Carbohydrates: 12g; Dietary Fiber: 2g; Protein: 2g

VERY DIRTY RICE
SERVES 3

Although most of the traditional ingredients are included in this recipe, chicken livers, which usually make dirty rice "dirty," are nowhere to be found in this or in many other versions of dirty rice. Here I have upped the usual vegetables and reduced the rice to make the dish lower in carbs and calories and higher in what I consider the dirt.

1 teaspoon olive oil
1 garlic clove, minced
1 bell pepper, any color is fine, diced
1 celery stalk, diced
1 Spanish or red onion, minced
1 small bunch scallions, chopped
¼ teaspoon dried oregano
¼ teaspoon dried thyme
1 teaspoon dried paprika
¼ teaspoon cayenne
⅔ cup white or brown rice
1 cup water
¼ cup chopped fresh Italian flat-leaf parsley leaves
1 teaspoon cider vinegar

■ Place a medium cast iron skillet over medium heat and when it is hot, add the oil. Add the garlic, bell pepper, celery, onion, scallions, oregano, thyme, paprika and cayenne and cook until tender, about 10 minutes. Add the rice and water and bring to a boil. Reduce the heat to low, cover and steam until the rice is tender, about 20 minutes. Add the parsley and cider vinegar and serve.

NUTRITION FACTS: Calories: 101; Calories from Fat: 13; Fat: 1.5g; Saturated Fat: 0g; Cholesterol: 0mg; Sodium: 7mg; Carbohydrates: 19.9g; Dietary Fiber: 1.8g; Protein: 2.2g

SALADS

TOMATO OLIVE SALAD
SERVES 3

This salad is best served when tomatoes are at their summertime peak, but if you can get really good tomatoes during other seasons, make this salad year-round. Although tomatoes are great just drizzled with olive oil, I have replaced the olive oil with these other very flavorful additions to add more depth.

8 cups chopped fresh tomatoes
¼ cup fresh basil leaves
2 tablespoons drained capers
3 tablespoons olive paste
2 garlic cloves, minced
¼ teaspoon black pepper

Place everything in a bowl and mix to combine. Serve immediately or cover and refrigerate up to overnight.

NUTRITION FACTS: Calories: 101; Calories from Fat: 26; Fat: 2.9g; Saturated Fat: 0g; Cholesterol: 0mg; Sodium: 192mg; Carbohydrates: 18.3g; Dietary Fiber: 5.6g; Protein: 4g

MIXED GREENS WITH HONEY VINAIGRETTE
SERVES 4

Although I am generally a fan of very tart dressings, this slightly sweet vinaigrette is a welcome break. This handy all-around dressing can be kept at the ready in the fridge (see below).

2 tablespoons olive oil
1½ tablespoons sherry vinegar
1 teaspoon honey
1 teaspoon Dijon mustard
½ teaspoon kosher salt
1 head romaine
2 bunches watercress
1 bunch arugula

Place the olive oil, vinegar, honey, mustard and salt in a small bowl and whisk until well combined. Place the lettuces in a salad bowl, add the vinaigrette and toss. Serve immediately.

TO MAKE 1 PINT VINAIGRETTE DRESSING:
1 cup olive oil
¾ cup sherry vinegar
2½ tablespoons honey
2½ tablespoons Dijon mustard
1 tablespoon kosher salt

NUTRITION FACTS: Calories: 100; Calories from Fat: 66; Fat: 7.4g; Saturated Fat: 1g; Cholesterol: 0mg; Sodium: 335mg; Carbohydrates: 7.5g; Dietary Fiber: 3.7g; Protein: 3g

CHICKPEA AND TOMATO SALAD

SERVES 6, ABOUT ⅓ CUP PER SERVING

Beans are high in calories yet so good and so filling. Chickpeas, so called for their little bump's resemblance to a chick's beak, are filled with vast health benefits: high in fiber, they help slow absorption of sugar (good for diabetics), high in calcium, magnesium, potassium and even protein.

1 can (15.5 ounces) chickpeas, drained and rinsed
1 large beefsteak tomato, diced
2 tablespoons plain low-fat yogurt
2 tablespoons chopped fresh Italian flat-leaf parsley leaves
1 tablespoon chopped fresh basil or cilantro leaves
1 tablespoon chopped fresh mint leaves
2 teaspoons fresh lemon juice
½ teaspoon fennel seed, crushed
1 garlic clove, minced
¼ teaspoon Dijon mustard
¼ to ½ teaspoon crushed red pepper flakes

■ Place everything in a bowl and mix to combine. Serve immediately or cover and refrigerate up to overnight.

NUTRITION FACTS: Calories: 97; Calories from Fat: 9; Fat: 1g; Saturated Fat: 0g; Cholesterol: 0mg; Sodium: 221mg; Carbohydrates: 18.3g; Dietary Fiber: 3.8g; Protein: 4.3g

ROMAINE LETTUCE SALAD WITH CHIVE VINAIGRETTE

SERVES 2

Although this salad is very simple, the sharp but delicate chives add a great fresh flavor to it. Feel free to add cucumbers, bell peppers or almost any other vegetable.

1 head romaine lettuce, torn into bite-size pieces
½ cup grape or cherry tomatoes
2 teaspoons olive oil
2 teaspoons fresh lemon juice
1 teaspoon Dijon mustard
3 to 4 tablespoons fresh chives, cut into
    1½ to 2 inch lengths
Kosher salt and black pepper

■ Place the lettuce in a serving bowl. Add the tomatoes. Place the oil, lemon juice and mustard in a small bowl and mix to combine. Add the chives and salt and pepper to taste. Pour over the lettuce and serve immediately.

NUTRITION FACTS: Calories: 101; Calories from Fat: 50; Fat: 5.6g; Saturated Fat: 0.8g; Cholesterol: 0mg; Sodium: 55mg; Carbohydrates: 11.8g; Dietary Fiber: 7g; Protein: 4.3g

BABY ARUGULA, BLOOD ORANGE AND BLUE CHEESE SALAD

SERVES 4

This is my perfect salad: arugula (also called rocket) is tender, mustardy and bitter sharp, a beautiful contrast to the juicy sweet orange and sharp, pungent blue cheese.

Aptly named for their crimson flesh, blood oranges are native to Italy and Spain. They are similar in taste to standard oranges, yet are often juicier and sweeter. Just like navel oranges, blood oranges provide more than 100 percent of your vitamin C requirement.

12 cups loosely packed baby arugula or regular arugula
1 large blood orange or 1 small grapefruit, peeled, seeded and thinly sliced
3 tablespoons crumbled blue cheese or feta cheese
Juice of 1 lemon
1 tablespoon plus 1 teaspoon olive oil
¼ to ½ teaspoon kosher salt

■ Place the arugula, orange and blue cheese in a large salad bowl. Drizzle with the lemon juice and olive oil and sprinkle with the salt. Toss lightly and serve immediately.

NUTRITION FACTS: Calories: 100; Calories from Fat: 61; Fat: 6.8g; Saturated Fat: 1.9g; Cholesterol: 5mg; Sodium: 250mg; Carbohydrates: 8.1g; Dietary Fiber: 2.1g; Protein: 3.3g

JICAMA SLAW
SERVES 6

Often referred to as "the Mexican potato," jicama is actually a member of the legume family. Resembling a large turnip, it has thin, gray skin and white flesh. When eaten raw, jicama tastes like a less-sweet version of a pear or apple, making it a perfect accompaniment to a raw vegetable platter.

1 jicama (1½ to 2 pounds), peeled and grated or very thinly julienned
2 carrots, grated
1 Granny Smith apple, peeled and grated
1 radicchio head, slivered
2 tablespoons olive oil
2 tablespoons fresh lime juice
1 teaspoon kosher salt
¼ teaspoon chili powder
¼ cup chopped fresh cilantro or basil leaves

■ Place the jicama, carrots and apple in a medium-size mixing bowl and toss well. Add the radicchio, olive oil, lime juice, salt and chili powder and toss well. Cover and refrigerate for at least 2 hours and up to overnight. Serve, garnished with the cilantro.

NUTRITION FACTS: Calories: 103; Calories from Fat: 42; Fat: 4.7g; Saturated Fat: 0.7g; Cholesterol: 0mg; Sodium: 407mg; Carbohydrates: 15.3g; Dietary Fiber: 6.5g; Protein: 1.1g

JERUSALEM ARTICHOKE SALAD WITH MUSTARD DRESSING

SERVES 4, ABOUT ½ CUP PER SERVING

Despite its name, the Jerusalem artichoke has no relation to either Jerusalem or to an artichoke. It is a member of the sunflower family and is often referred to as a sunchoke. When raw, its white flesh has a nutty flavor; when cooked it tastes similar to an artichoke heart.

- **1½ teaspoons minced shallot**
- **1 tablespoon coarse grain mustard**
- **1 tablespoon cider vinegar**
- **1 tablespoon canola or olive oil**
- **1 pound (2 cups) Jerusalem artichokes, scrubbed ruthlessly, trimmed and thinly sliced**
- **1 bunch watercress, trimmed, rinsed and dried**

■ Place the shallot, mustard and vinegar in a small bowl and whisk to combine. Gradually whisk in the oil. Add the Jerusalem artichokes to the bowl, mix, cover, and refrigerate for 30 minutes to 1 hour. Serve on a bed of watercress.

NUTRITION FACTS: Calories: 91; Calories from Fat: 33; Fat: 3.6g; Saturated Fat: .9g; Cholesterol: 0mg; Sodium: 27mg; Carbohydrates: 13.7g; Dietary Fiber: 1.2g; Protein: 1.7g

BEET AND BEET GREEN SALAD
SERVES 4

I am a huge fan of beets but hate to throw away the nutritious greens, so I developed this salad that uses both. Additionally, the greens serve to cut some of the sweetness of the beets.

¼ teaspoon kosher salt
1½ pounds beets (of uniform size) including greens (to yield about 2 cups beet greens and ¾ pound beets)
1 orange, peeled, seeded and sliced into thin sections
¼ red onion, thinly sliced
1 teaspoon olive oil
1 teaspoon red wine vinegar
2 tablespoons feta cheese

■ Place a large pot of water over high heat and bring to a boil. Add the salt and then the beets (but not the beet greens) and return to a boil. Reduce the heat to low, cover, and cook until the beets are tender when pierced with a fork, 20 to 40 minutes, depending upon the size of the beets. Set aside until cool enough to handle. Slice or cut into large dice.
■ Place the beet greens in a large salad bowl. Add the orange, onion, oil and vinegar. Toss well. Add the beets and toss again. Add the feta and serve immediately.

NUTRITION FACTS: Calories: 98; Calories from Fat: 21; Fat: 2.3g; Saturated Fat: 0.9g; Cholesterol: 4mg; Sodium: 435mg; Carbohydrates: 17.3g; Dietary Fiber: 25.6g; Protein: 4.1g

RADISH CUCUMBER SALAD

SERVES 2, ABOUT 2 CUPS PER SERVING

When I was growing up my mother often put radishes in her salads. I found the sharp peppery flavor too much, but now love them and add them to my salads, which my children, in turn, pick out.

2 cups sliced or diced radishes
2 cups sliced or diced English cucumbers
½ cup chopped red onion
2½ teaspoons olive oil
2 teaspoons fresh lemon or lime juice
¼ cup chopped fresh cilantro leaves
¼ teaspoon kosher salt
¼ teaspoon crushed red pepper flakes

■ Place everything in a bowl and mix to combine. Serve immediately or cover and refrigerate up to overnight.

NUTRITION FACTS: Calories: 98; Calories from Fat: 54; Fat: 5.9g; Saturated Fat: 0.9g; Cholesterol: 0mg; Sodium: 340mg; Carbohydrates: 11g; Dietary Fiber: 3.1g; Protein: 1.9g

CARROT SLAW
SERVES 2

Sweet, crunchy, light and incredibly easy to make, this is the salad to have on hand all the time. Don't be tempted to dispense with the oil: the carotenoids in carrots are best absorbed when paired with a little bit of fat.

½ **pound carrots (about 4), shredded**
Juice of ½ lemon
2 teaspoons olive oil
1 tablespoon currants

■ Place everything in a bowl and mix to combine. Serve immediately or cover and refrigerate up to overnight.

NUTRITION FACTS: Calories: 90; Calories from Fat: 43; Fat: 4.8g; Saturated Fat: 0.7g; Cholesterol: 0mg; Sodium: 78mg; Carbohydrates: 12g; Dietary Fiber: 3.4g; Protein: 1.1g

GREEK SALAD

SERVES 4

A dding spinach to the classic Greek salad adds a depth and interest that I really like. Be sure to use with baby spinach or bunch spinach, which is much tastier and fresher than the curly spinach found bagged in most markets.

1 head romaine lettuce, pale green inner leaves only
3 cups baby spinach leaves
1 beefsteak tomato, cubed
½ English cucumber, cubed
1 small red onion, thinly sliced
1½ tablespoons olive oil
1½ tablespoons fresh lemon juice
1 teaspoon dried Greek oregano
½ teaspoon kosher salt
¼ teaspoon black pepper
¼ cup crumbled feta cheese

■ Place the romaine, spinach, tomato, cucumber and red onion in a large salad bowl and toss to combine. Place the oil, lemon juice, oregano, salt and pepper in a small bowl and whisk together. Pour over the salad, gently toss, sprinkle with the feta cheese, and serve.

NUTRITION FACTS: Calories: 104; Calories from Fat: 67; Fat: 7.4g; Saturated Fat: 2.2g; Cholesterol: 8mg; Sodium: 424mg; Carbohydrates: 8g; Dietary Fiber: 2.4g; Protein: 3.4g

ITALIAN TRICOLOR

SERVES 2

Arugula, endive and radicchio, the classic Italian trio of lettuces, are all considered slightly bitter but so beloved by me. See the recipe measures below if you want to make a big batch of the dressing and keep it on hand in the refrigerator.

1½ teaspoons olive oil
1 teaspoon fresh lemon juice
⅛ teaspoon anchovy paste
⅛ teaspoon Dijon mustard
½ bunch arugula
1 head endive, chopped
½ head radicchio, chopped
2 tablespoons shaved Parmesan cheese

■ Place the olive oil, lemon juice, anchovy paste and mustard in a small bowl and mix well. Place the arugula, endive and radicchio in a bowl, add the dressing, and gently toss. Garnish with the Parmesan.

TO MAKE A LARGE BATCH OF DRESSING:
1½ cups olive oil
1 cup fresh lemon juice
1 tablespoon anchovy paste
1 tablespoon Dijon mustard

NUTRITION FACTS: Calories: 103; Calories from Fat: 49; Fat: 5.4g; Saturated Fat: 1.5g; Cholesterol: 4mg; Sodium: 144mg; Carbohydrates: 10.3g; Dietary Fiber: 8.3g; Protein: 5.7g

WATERMELON AND FETA SALAD

SERVES 4

The salad of the moment but so good, it should last forever.

Although high in sugar, watermelon also contains a high concentration of antioxidants, specifically those that help to protect against diabetes, colon cancer and arthritis. Additionally, watermelon boasts a good amount of lycopene, an antioxidant most notably found in tomatoes, which has been proven to lower the risk of breast and lung cancer.

6 cups cubed and seeded watermelon
1½ cups cubed cucumber
¼ cup crumbled feta cheese
16 grape tomatoes, halved or left whole
Juice of 1 lime
½ teaspoon kosher salt
¼ teaspoon black pepper
¼ cup chopped fresh basil or mint leaves
1 lime, quartered

■ Place everything, except the lime, in a bowl and mix to combine. Serve immediately or cover and refrigerate up to overnight. Garnish with the lime quarters.

NUTRITION FACTS: Calories: 105; Calories from Fat: 22; Fat: 2.5g; Saturated Fat: 1.5g; Cholesterol: 8mg; Sodium: 401mg; Carbohydrates: 20.3g; Dietary Fiber: 1.7g; Protein: 3.3g

ASPARAGUS SALAD WITH GOAT CHEESE AND TARRAGON

SERVES 4

Widely used in French cooking, tarragon, a member of the sunflower family, has a slightly bittersweet anise flavor that nicely complements the asparagus. There are two cultivated species of tarragon, Russian and French. Tarragon, unlike many other herbs, was used as a medicinal drug until the sixteenth century and was not brought to the United States until the early nineteenth century. It was believed to cure snakebite.

- 1 tablespoon extra-virgin olive oil
- 1 tablespoon red wine vinegar
- 2 teaspoons Dijon mustard
- 1 teaspoon kosher salt
- ½ teaspoon black pepper
- 4 cups mesclun greens
- 20 asparagus spears, trimmed, blanched, shocked and cut into big chunks
- 1 pint cherry tomatoes, left whole or halved
- 2 tablespoons crumbled goat cheese
- 1 tablespoon coarsely chopped fresh tarragon leaves

■ Place the olive oil, vinegar, mustard, salt and pepper in a small bowl and mix to combine. Divide the mesclun greens among 4 salad plates and top with equal amounts of asparagus and tomatoes. Top with the goat cheese and tarragon and drizzle with the dressing.

NUTRITION FACTS: Calories: 104; Calories from Fat: 57; Fat: 6.3g; Saturated Fat: 2.3g; Cholesterol: 7mg; Sodium: 644mg; Carbohydrates: 8.2g; Dietary Fiber: 3.7g; Protein: 5.8g

RED CABBAGE WITH ASIAN DRESSING
SERVES 5, ABOUT 2 CUPS PER SERVING

Crunchy, colorful and clean tasting, it's hard not to feel virtuous when you eat this stunning and substantial salad. Red cabbage produces a slaw with a stronger taste than green, but if you are looking for something more delicate, you can readily substitute green or savoy cabbage. If you want some spice in your slaw, add crushed red pepper flakes.

2 tablespoons canola oil
2 tablespoons seasoned rice wine vinegar
Pinch sugar
1 teaspoon kosher salt
1 teaspoon black pepper
1 head red cabbage, shredded
2 carrots, cut into julienne
8 scallions, finely sliced

■ Place the oil, vinegar, sugar, salt and pepper in a small bowl and whisk to combine. Place the cabbage, carrots and scallions in a large bowl and toss well. Add the dressing and toss again. Cover and refrigerate for at least 1 hour and up to 2 days.

NUTRITION FACTS: Calories: 99; Calories from Fat: 52; Fat: 5.8g; Saturated Fat: 0g; Cholesterol: 0mg; Sodium: 532mg; Carbohydrates: 11.4g; Dietary Fiber: 4.4g; Protein: 2.1g

HEARTS OF PALM SALAD

SERVES 4

As the name implies, hearts of palm are harvested from the inner core of certain palm trees. Often sold in cans, they make an excellent addition to salads or as an accompaniment on vegetable platters. The translucent white flesh has a mild nutty flavor, similar to that of a water chestnut.

8 hearts of palm, halved lengthwise
4 beefsteak tomatoes, sliced or diced
¼ red onion, thinly sliced
1 tablespoon olive oil
1 tablespoon fresh lemon juice
2 teaspoons Dijon mustard
4 scallions, chopped
¼ cup chopped fresh basil leaves

■ Place everything in a bowl and mix to combine. Serve immediately or cover and refrigerate up to overnight.

NUTRITION FACTS: Calories: 83; Calories from Fat: 38; Fat: 4.2g; Saturated Fat: 0.6g; Cholesterol: 0mg; Sodium: 348mg; Carbohydrates: 10.4g; Dietary Fiber: 3.9g; Protein: 3.4g

TOMATO AND PEACH SALAD
SERVES 2

The combination of tomato, peach and curry is truly sublime. Even if tomatoes had no nutritional value, I'd gratefully eat them, but they are also filled with nutrients that protect against almost all cancers (most notably stomach, prostate and lung). They are also high in lutein (good for eyes), which is best absorbed when eaten with a little bit of fat.

- 2 perfectly ripe peaches, cored and diced
- 2 beefsteak tomatoes, diced
- 2 tablespoons chopped fresh basil leaves
- 2 teaspoons olive oil
- 2 teaspoons orange juice
- ½ teaspoon curry powder
- ½ teaspoon kosher salt

■ Place everything in a bowl and mix to combine. Serve immediately or cover and refrigerate up to overnight.

NUTRITION FACTS: Calories: 105; Calories from Fat: 46; Fat: 5.1g; Saturated Fat: 0.7g; Cholesterol: 0mg; Sodium: 588mg; Carbohydrates: 15.1g; Dietary Fiber: 3.2g; Protein: 2.2g

ICEBERG QUARTERS WITH BLUE CHEESE

SERVES 4

I ceberg lettuce seems to go in and out of favor but sometimes nothing can beat it for texture and crunch, and its very simplicity makes it a great vehicle for many flavors. This is a great salad to make when you have a grill going: throw the lettuce wedges on and grill them briefly. It may sound bizarre but it's delicious.

⅓ **cup blue cheese, mashed**
½ **cup buttermilk**
1 small garlic clove, minced
1 teaspoon fresh lemon juice
1 head iceberg lettuce, cut into 4 wedges
8 cherry tomatoes
Fresh chives

■ Place the blue cheese in a small bowl and gradually add the buttermilk, mashing after each addition. When it is mostly incorporated, add the garlic and lemon juice.
■ Place the lettuce wedges on serving plates and top with the dressing, tomatoes and chives.

NUTRITION FACTS: Calories: 98; Calories from Fat: 36; Fat: 4g; Saturated Fat: 2.3g; Cholesterol: 10mg; Sodium: 207mg; Carbohydrates: 11.7g; Dietary Fiber: 3.2g; Protein: 5.8g

VEGETABLES

JALAPEÑO SPINACH

SERVES 1

Spinach has only 7 calories per cup, is packed with essential nutrients like calcium, iron and vitamin A, and supplies a host of health benefits. Not only does it improve bone strength, but it also improves eyesight and mental functions, and helps prevent heart disease. It's no wonder spinach was Popeye's food of choice.

½ **teaspoon olive oil**
2 garlic cloves, chopped
1 jalapeño pepper, thinly sliced
⅔ **pound fresh flat-leaf spinach, ends trimmed and
 discarded, leaves washed and not dried well**
⅛ **teaspoon kosher salt**
Pinch black pepper

■ Place a large skillet over medium heat and when it is hot, add the olive oil. Add the garlic and jalapeño and cook, stirring, until the garlic is golden, 3 to 5 minutes. Add a quarter of the spinach and cook, stirring, until it has wilted somewhat, 1 to 2 minutes. Continue adding spinach, about a quarter at a time, and cook, stirring, until it has all wilted. Add the salt and pepper.

NUTRITION FACTS: Calories: 103; Calories from Fat: 32; Fat: 3.5g; Saturated Fat: 0.5g; Cholesterol: 0mg; Sodium: 531mg; Carbohydrates: 13.8g; Dietary Fiber: 7.2g; Protein: 9.2g

FRESH TOMATO AND HERB COMPOTE
SERVES 4

lthough this luscious compote makes a great side dish, it's satisfying on its own. When tomatoes are ripe, I often make a big batch to freeze in small containers for quick future microwaving.

1 tablespoon olive oil
¼ cup finely chopped red onion
1 garlic clove, minced
4 beefsteak tomatoes, diced
3 tablespoons finely chopped fresh Italian flat-leaf parsley leaves
3 tablespoons finely chopped fresh oregano leaves
½ teaspoon kosher salt
½ teaspoon ground black pepper
2 tablespoons pine nuts, toasted

■ Place a large cast iron skillet over high heat and when it is hot, add the oil. Add the onion and garlic and cook, stirring, until the onion starts to lose its red color and just slightly browns, about 5 minutes. Add the tomatoes, parsley, oregano, salt and pepper and cook, stirring, until the tomatoes are heated through, about 2 minutes. Stir in the pine nuts and serve.

NUTRITION FACTS: Calories: 97; Calories from Fat: 63; Fat: 6.9g; Saturated Fat: 0.8g; Cholesterol: 0mg; Sodium: 300mg; Carbohydrates: 8.8g; Dietary Fiber: 3.4g; Protein: 2.3g

SUMMER SQUASH, CORN AND TOMATO SAUTÉ

SERVES 4

Unquestionably summer's quintessential sauté, best made when all the ingredients are at their peak!

2 teaspoons olive oil
½ red onion, chopped
3 garlic cloves, minced
3 pattypan or other summer squash, cubed
2 ears of corn, kernels scraped off
3 beefsteak tomatoes, diced
¼ teaspoon kosher salt
2 tablespoons chopped fresh basil leaves

■ Place a large cast iron skillet over high heat and when it is hot, add the oil. Add the onion and garlic and cook, stirring, until the onion starts to lose its red color and just slightly browns, about 5 minutes. Add the squash and cook until it is tender and just starts to brown, about 12 minutes. Add the corn kernels, tomatoes and salt and cook, stirring, until heated through, about 5 minutes. Serve immediately, garnished with the basil.

NUTRITION FACTS: Calories: 101; Calories from Fat: 28; Fat: 3.2g; Saturated Fat: 0g; Cholesterol: 0mg; Sodium: 171mg; Carbohydrates: 17.5g; Dietary Fiber: 4g; Protein: 4.1g

OVEN-ROASTED PARSNIPS
SERVES 4

A root vegetable originally as popular as the potato, the parsnip is a yellowish, fruity carrot-like vegetable that is a little bit nutty and when raw, almost cloyingly sweet. It's definitely best roasted.

1 pound parsnips, cut into spears
1 teaspoon olive oil
½ teaspoon chili or curry powder
½ teaspoon kosher salt

■ Preheat the oven to 425°F. Place everything in a bowl, toss well, and place on a baking sheet. Transfer to the oven and roast until the parsnips are golden brown, about 20 minutes. Serve immediately.

NUTRITION FACTS: Calories: 96; Calories from Fat: 14; Fat: 1.5g; Saturated Fat: 0g; Cholesterol: 0mg; Sodium: 306mg; Carbohydrates: 20.5g; Dietary Fiber: 5.6g; Protein: 1.4g

BROCCOLI RABE WITH DRIED CRANBERRIES AND FETA CHEESE

SERVES 2

To properly describe broccoli rabe—one of my preferred vegetables—you must say it is bitter and peppery, which just doesn't do it justice. This particular dish, which can be served hot or cold, is a great introduction to broccoli rabe, as the cranberries and feta cheese mellow its strong flavor.

1 bunch broccoli rabe
¼ cup water
1½ tablespoons dried cranberries
1 ounce feta cheese, crumbled

■ Place a large nonstick skillet over medium heat and add the rabe and water. Cook until the rabe brightens, about 7 minutes. Transfer to a plate, add the cranberries and feta cheese, and eat!

NUTRITION FACTS: Calories: 98; Calories from Fat: 27; Fat: 3g; Saturated Fat: 2.1g; Cholesterol: 13mg; Sodium: 200mg; Carbohydrates: 12g; Dietary Fiber: 0g; Protein: 6.2g

LEMONY GREEN AND WHITE BEANS

SERVES 4, ABOUT ⅔ CUP PER SERVING

The combination of creamy white beans, crunchy green beans and sharp mustard make this pretty salad a favorite.

1½ cups canned white beans, drained and rinsed well
2 cups fresh green beans, halved
1 scallion, chopped
1 teaspoon Dijon mustard
½ teaspoon fresh lemon juice
Freshly grated zest of ½ lemon
½ teaspoon anchovy paste

■ Place all the ingredients in a medium-size bowl and toss well. Cover and refrigerate for at least 1 hour and up to overnight.

NUTRITION FACTS: Calories: 102; Calories from Fat: 1; Fat: 0.1g; Saturated Fat: 0g; Cholesterol: 0mg; Sodium: 40mg; Carbohydrates: 19g; Dietary Fiber: 6g; Protein: 7.1g

RATATOUILLE

SERVES 4

After I reduced the oil in ratatouille, a simple French Provençal dish, I actually preferred it to the original over-oily rendition. The flavor of the vegetables is sharper and cleaner. It's a great side dish or snack, hot or cold, but can also be used to top a burger or fill an omelet.

1 teaspoon olive oil
1 Spanish or red onion, chopped
1 red bell pepper, diced
4 garlic cloves, minced
1 medium eggplant, peeled, if desired, and diced
2 zucchini, diced
2 cups diced tomatoes, canned or fresh
1 lemon, quartered
2 tablespoons finely grated Parmesan cheese
2 tablespoons chopped fresh basil leaves

■ Place a large skillet over medium heat and when it is hot, add the oil. Add the onion, red pepper and garlic and cook, stirring occasionally, for 10 minutes. Add the eggplant and zucchini, cover, and cook, stirring occasionally, for 15 minutes more. Add the tomatoes and cook, uncovered, stirring occasionally, for 10 minutes if they are canned, or 20 minutes, if fresh.

■ Cover and refrigerate overnight or serve immediately, garnished with the lemon quarters, Parmesan cheese and basil.

NUTRITION FACTS: Calories: 100; Calories from Fat: 22; Fat: 2.5g; Saturated Fat: 0.7g; Cholesterol: 2mg; Sodium: 56mg; Carbohydrates: 17.7g; Dietary Fiber: 6.9g; Protein: 4.7g

GARLICKY ASPARAGUS WITH ANCHOVY
SERVES 2

This simple recipe could make an asparagus eater out of anyone.

1¼ **pounds asparagus, woody stems discarded, remainder halved**
1 **teaspoon olive oil**
3 **garlic cloves, minced**
1 **anchovy fillet, minced**
1 **tablespoon panko bread crumbs**
½ **teaspoon kosher salt**
¼ **teaspoon black pepper**
1 **tablespoon fresh lemon juice**

▓ Place a large pot of water over high heat and when it is boiling, add the asparagus. Allow to boil until bright green, about 4 minutes. Drain and rinse with ice water. Set aside.
▓ Place a small skillet over high heat and when it is hot, add the oil. Add the garlic and anchovy and cook, stirring, until the garlic is just starting to color, about 2 minutes. Add the asparagus and panko bread crumbs and cook until it just starts to get some golden flecks, 1 to 2 minutes. Add the salt and pepper and stir. Add the lemon juice and serve.

NUTRITION FACTS: Calories: 99; Calories from Fat: 25; Fat: 2.8g; Saturated Fat: 0g; Cholesterol: 0mg; Sodium: 613mg; Carbohydrates: 15.7g; Dietary Fiber: 6.3g; Protein: 7g

CREAMY ROASTED MUSHROOMS
SERVES 4

Mushrooms are mostly water, so when you start this recipe you will surely think you're making enough for an army, but they shrink down considerably. I never really liked mushrooms until I started roasting them: hands down, it's the best way to extract flavor and get the best texture. The cream adds very few calories but nicely smoothes out the flavor and texture.

2 pounds button mushrooms, halved and sliced
1 pound fresh shiitake mushroom, sliced
½ pound fresh oyster mushrooms, sliced
2 teaspoons kosher salt
2 teaspoons fresh rosemary leaves, chopped
1 tablespoon heavy cream

■ Preheat the oven to 400°F. Place the mushrooms and salt on 2 baking pans, toss well and transfer to the oven. After 10 minutes, remove the pans from the oven, add the rosemary, and mix the mushrooms around. Return to the oven until just golden, about 10 additional minutes. Remove from the oven, add the cream, stir well, and serve.

NUTRITION FACTS: Calories: 102; Calories from Fat: 25; Fat: 2.8g; Saturated Fat: 1.1g; Cholesterol: 5mg; Sodium: 1184mg; Carbohydrates: 13.5g; Dietary Fiber: 4.2g; Protein: 12.4g

SILKY, CREAMY BUTTERNUT SQUASH
SERVES 2

This is so good, so silky, so rich, and so lush, it's almost like eating dessert.

5 cups peeled, cubed butternut squash
½ tablespoon unsalted butter
1 tablespoon heavy cream
1 teaspoon kosher salt
1 tablespoon nonfat Greek yogurt (optional)
1 teaspoon chopped fresh basil leaves (optional)

■ Place the butternut squash and 2 inches of water in a large pot and bring to a boil over high heat. Reduce the heat to low, cover, and simmer until the squash is tender, about 15 minutes. Drain and mash. Add the butter, cream and salt and stir well. Serve garnished with the yogurt and basil, if desired.

NUTRITION FACTS: Calories: 97; Calories from Fat: 55; Fat: 6.2g; Saturated Fat: 3.7g; Cholesterol: 18mg; Sodium: 1214mg; Carbohydrates: 9.7g; Dietary Fiber: 3.1g; Protein: 3.6g

STUFFED ZUCCHINI BOATS
SERVES 4

One of these boats is not just a great snack, it's enough for lunch! You can make several ahead of time and eat them all week: you can either reheat at 400°F for about 5 minutes or in the microwave, although I have been known to eat them right out of the fridge.

4 medium-size zucchini, halved lengthwise, one half chopped, other half hollowed out
1 beefsteak tomato, diced
⅓ cup panko bread crumbs
3 tablespoons farmer cheese
2 tablespoons finely shredded Parmesan cheese
2 tablespoons chopped fresh basil leaves
½ teaspoon dried oregano
½ teaspoon kosher salt
¼ teaspoon black pepper

■ Preheat the oven to 400°F. Lightly coat an 8 x 8-inch baking pan with spray. Place the hollowed out zucchini halves (there should be 4, not 8) in the prepared baking pan.
■ Place the chopped zucchini, tomato, panko bread crumbs, farmer and Parmesan cheeses, basil, oregano, salt and pepper in a large bowl and stir to combine. Divide the mixture between the zucchini halves. Transfer to the oven and bake until the zucchini is tender and the top is browned, about 40 minutes.

NUTRITION FACTS: Calories: 100; Calories from Fat: 23; Fat: 2.5g; Saturated Fat: 1.2g; Cholesterol: 6mg; Sodium: 460mg; Carbohydrates: 14g; Dietary Fiber: 2.9g; Protein: 6.6g

STEAMED CORN WITH CHILI "BUTTER"

SERVES 4

Because of its high starch content, corn is very filling. Though this makes a great side dish at a meal, corn shouldn't be overlooked as a snack, particularly during the summer.

4 medium ears of corn
2 tablespoons water
2½ teaspoons unsalted butter or olive oil
1 teaspoon ground chipotle chili powder
1 teaspoon kosher salt
1 lime, quartered

■ Place the corn, water, butter, chili powder and salt in a large skillet and bring to a boil over high heat. Cover and cook, turning once, until the corn is tender and the water has evaporated, about 5 minutes. Roll the corn in the butter mixture and serve immediately, garnished with lime.

NUTRITION FACTS: Calories: 100; Calories from Fat: 31; Fat: 3.5g; Saturated Fat: 1.7g; Cholesterol: 6mg; Sodium: 31mg; Carbohydrates: 17.4g; Dietary Fiber: 2.5g; Protein: 3g

BOK CHOY WITH SESAME
SERVES 1

Also known as Chinese cabbage, bok choy is a leafy, mild green vegetable often used in Asian cooking. Its white stalks are stringy and bear a slight resemblance to celery, while its green leaves are akin to romaine lettuce. Most often bok choy is braised or boiled before being eaten. High in calcium, potassium, beta carotene and vitamin A, bok choy has only 15 calories per cup!

4 baby bok choy (about 3 ounces each)
1 cup chicken stock
4 teaspoons low-sodium soy sauce
½ teaspoon toasted sesame oil
¼ teaspoon black pepper

■ Place the bok choy and chicken stock in a large skillet and bring to a boil over high heat. Reduce the heat and cook until the bok choy is tender, about 5 minutes. Transfer to a plate.
■ Reheat the liquid in the skillet, add the soy sauce and sesame oil and cook until the liquid has reduced to ½ cup. Drizzle the sauce over the bok choy, season with the pepper, and serve.

NUTRITION FACTS: Calories: 101; Calories from Fat: 37; Fat: 4.1g; Saturated Fat: 0.8g; Cholesterol: 0mg; Sodium: 2110mg; Carbohydrates: 8g; Dietary Fiber: 2.6g; Protein: 9.7g

ROASTED SWEET POTATO FRIES

SERVES 1

Sweet potatoes are a great creamy, sweet yet healthy treat. Their size range is huge so be sure to weigh yours: a large sweet potato can weigh up to three times what a small sweet potato weighs.

1 small sweet potato (about 4 ounces), cut into 8 spears
½ teaspoon kosher salt
⅛ teaspoon ground nutmeg
⅛ teaspoon olive oil

Preheat the oven to 400°F. Place all the ingredients in a small bowl and toss until the sweet potatoes are well coated. Pour onto a pan and transfer to the oven. Roast until the sweet potatoes are darkened on the outside and soft on the inside, about 30 minutes. Serve immediately.

NUTRITION FACTS: Calories: 96; Calories from Fat: 7; Fat: 0.8g; Saturated Fat: 0g; Cholesterol: 0mg; Sodium: 617mg; Carbohydrates: 20.8g; Dietary Fiber: 3.3g; Protein: 2g

PROTEIN

CUCUMBER AND SHRIMP SALAD #1

SERVES 1

Slightly Asian in flavor and high in protein, this light salad is satisfying enough for lunch. Although I think fresh shrimp is best, I keep a bag in my freezer for easy access.

1 cup very thin cucumber slices
6 large shrimp (21/25 shrimp), cooked, cooled and sliced through the center
2 tablespoons seasoned rice wine vinegar
1 x 1-inch piece nori
Juice and freshly grated zest of ½ lime
¼ teaspoon kosher salt
¼ teaspoon sugar
¼ teaspoon minced or shredded fresh gingerroot

■ Place everything in a small bowl, gently toss and serve immediately or cover and refrigerate overnight.

NUTRITION FACTS: Calories: 99; Calories from Fat: 8; Fat: 0.9g; Saturated Fat: 0g; Cholesterol: 133mg; Sodium: 856mg; Carbohydrates: 7.3g; Dietary Fiber: 0.6g; Protein: 14.9

CUCUMBER AND SHRIMP SALAD #2

SERVES 1

The combination of the amazingly low-calorie cucumber with the amazingly low-calorie shrimp creates an almost nonfat, filling and nutritious Japanese-inspired salad.

1 cup thinly sliced English cucumbers
9 large shrimp (21/25 shrimp), peeled, cooked and cooled
2 tablespoons seasoned rice vinegar
1 x 1-inch piece of nori
1 teaspoon low-sodium soy sauce
¼ teaspoon kosher salt
¼ teaspoon sugar
¼ teaspoon minced fresh gingerroot

▨ Place everything in a bowl and mix to combine. Serve immediately or cover and refrigerate up to overnight.

NUTRITION FACTS: Calories: 100; Calories from Fat: 8; Fat: 0.9g; Saturated Fat: 0g; Cholesterol: 133mg; Sodium: 1155mg; Carbohydrates: 7.3g; Dietary Fiber: 0.6g; Protein: 15.2g

SMOKED SALMON WITH ASPARAGUS

Serves 1

Though quite light, this high-protein salad is very filling. If you are going to take it with you to work, you can make it ahead of time and leave out the lemon juice. Add the lemon juice just before serving.

1 ounce smoked salmon, sliced
6 asparagus spears, steamed and cooled
½ cup thinly sliced cucumbers
¼ cup thinly sliced red onion
1 teaspoon lemon juice
½ teaspoon olive oil
Pinch salt
Pinch black pepper

■ Place everything in a small bowl, gently toss and serve immediately or cover and refrigerate overnight.

NUTRITION FACTS: Calories: 102; Calories from Fat: 34; Fat: 3.7g; Saturated Fat: 0.7g; Cholesterol: 7mg; Sodium: 572mg; Carbohydrates: 10.6g; Dietary Fiber: 3.8g; Protein: 9g

GREEN BEANS AND TOFU

SERVES 1

Made from the coagulation of soy milk, tofu is often used as a vegetarian alternative to beef or chicken. While it has little flavor on its own, it is a great vehicle for a variety of marinades and seasonings. Low in calories and high in protein, tofu is an excellent choice for both snacks and entrées.

- **1 cup green beans, halved, steamed and cooled**
- **⅕ of a 1-pound block silken tofu (⅕ pound, 3.2 ounces), diced**
- **4 fresh basil leaves, julienned**
- **1 teaspoon seasoned rice vinegar**
- **1 teaspoon low-sodium soy sauce**
- **¼ teaspoon grated fresh gingerroot**
- **1 tablespoon red bell pepper slivers**
- **⅛ teaspoon lightly toasted sesame seeds**

■ Place everything in a small bowl, gently toss and serve immediately or cover and refrigerate overnight.

NUTRITION FACTS: Calories: 101; Calories from Fat: 25; Fat: 2.8g; Saturated Fat: 0g; Cholesterol: 0mg; Sodium: 216mg; Carbohydrates: 11.4g; Dietary Fiber: 4.2g; Protein: 8.7g

SCALLOP SEVICHE
SERVES 2

Seviche, ceviche, cebiche—whatever you call this Latin American dish, it's always a combination of raw fish, citrus (most often lime) and vegetables. The amount of time you marinate is a matter of preference, but since I don't like what the citrus does to the texture of the scallops—they lose their wonderful creaminess after 2 hours—I suggest a shorter marinating time than most recipes call for.

⅓ **pound bay scallops**
½ **beefsteak tomato, diced**
¼ **small red onion, chopped**
⅛ **avocado, diced**
1 teaspoon fresh lime juice
2 teaspoons chopped fresh cilantro leaves, plus additional for garnish
1 tablespoon fresh orange juice
1 scallion greens, finely sliced
Vietnamese chili paste or jalapeño pepper, chopped (optional)

■ Place everything in a large glass or ceramic bowl, cover and refrigerate for at least 1 hour and no more than 2 hours. Garnish with additional cilantro.

NUTRITION FACTS: Calories: 102; Calories from Fat: 23; Fat: 2.5g; Saturated Fat: 0g; Cholesterol: 25mg; Sodium: 126mg; Carbohydrates: 6.5g; Dietary Fiber: 1.6g; Protein: 13.5g

SMOKED TURKEY WRAPPED IN ROMAINE LETTUCE

SERVES 1

Feel free to substitute fresh or pepper turkey for the smoked turkey. If you choose maple or honey turkey, just be sure to read the nutrition label and reduce the amount accordingly.

1 romaine lettuce leaf
½ teaspoon Dijon mustard
2½ ounces smoked turkey
4 thin slices cucumber
2 tomato slices

■ Hollow out the seeds from 1 cucumber slice Place the romaine on a flat surface and make it as flat as possible. Brush with the mustard and then top with the smoked turkey and remaining 3 cucumber slices. Roll into a cylinder and slip into the hollowed-out cucumber slice. Serve garnished with the tomato slices.

NUTRITION FACTS: Calories: 92; Calories from Fat: 27; Fat: 3g; Saturated Fat: 0.9g; Cholesterol: 45mg; Sodium: 674mg; Carbohydrates: 3.8g; Dietary Fiber: 0g; Protein: 12g

SHRIMP WITH SPICED SALT

SERVES 1

This recipe offers a lot of shrimp and a lot of protein for a 100-calorie snack or quick lunch. You can use any size shrimp you like but just be sure to check the weight. The recipe makes a lot more salt than you need for the recipe, but you can keep it stored in a jar in the spice cabinet and save it for the next time you make the recipe.

11 large shrimp (.2 pound), boiled, grilled or broiled

SPICED SALT (7 calories per teaspoon)
2 tablespoons chili powder
2 teaspoons garlic powder
2 teaspoons dried oregano
2 teaspoons kosher salt
1 teaspoon ground cumin

1 lime quarter

■ Place the shrimp on a plate. In a bowl, mix together the Spiced Salt ingredients. Sprinkle as much of the salt as desired over the shrimp. Garnish with the lime quarter.

NUTRITION FACTS (for the shrimp only): Calories: 90; Calories from Fat: 9; Fat: 1g; Saturated Fat: 0g; Cholesterol: 177mg; Sodium: 203mg; Carbohydrates: 0g; Dietary Fiber: 0g; Protein: 19g

CURRIED TUNA

SERVES 3

As long as you have most of the ingredients on hand, curried tuna is another high protein, easy snack you can readily prepare. I keep several cans of tuna in the fridge so that the salad chills faster.

- 1 tablespoon Greek or plain low-fat yogurt
- 1 tablespoon reduced calorie mayonnaise
- 1 tablespoon mango chutney
- 1 teaspoon curry powder
- 1 can (6½ ounces) white tuna in water, drained well
- 1 celery stick, chopped
- 1 small Granny Smith or Pink Lady apple, cut in small dice
- 2 tablespoons chopped fresh cilantro or basil leaves, plus additional for garnish

■ Place everything in a small bowl and gently mix. Transfer to a container, cover and refrigerate for at least 1 hour and up to overnight.

NUTRITION FACTS: Calories: 101; Calories from Fat: 22; Fat: 2.4g; Saturated Fat: 0.6g; Cholesterol: 20mg; Sodium: 108mg; Carbohydrates: 8.6g; Dietary Fiber: 1.1g; Protein: 11.4g

ASPARAGUS AND SCALLOPS OVER GREENS

SERVES 2

Special enough for a lunch to impress. Your guest will never know they are eating so low calorie!

¼ teaspoon olive oil
½ garlic clove, thinly sliced or minced
6 ounces scallops, dried with a paper towel
⅛ teaspoon Hungarian or smoked paprika
¼ teaspoon kosher salt
Pinch black pepper
6 asparagus spears, trimmed, blanched for a minute in simmering water and cut into 1-inch chunks
½ teaspoon fresh thyme leaves
1 teaspoon fresh lemon juice
1½ cups mesclun greens

■ Place a large skillet over medium heat and when it is hot, add the oil. Add the garlic and cook, stirring, until soft and golden, about 3 minutes. Sprinkle the scallops with the paprika, salt and pepper and add them to the skillet. Cook until browned on all sides, 3 to 4 minutes total. Stir in the asparagus and cook until heated. Add the thyme and lemon juice.

■ Divide the greens between 2 salad plates and top with equal amounts of the scallop mixture. Serve immediately.

NUTRITION FACTS: Calories: 100; Calories from Fat: 12; Fat: 1.4g; Saturated Fat: 0g; Cholesterol: 28mg; Sodium: 433mg; Carbohydrates: 6.2g; Dietary Fiber: 1.9g; Protein: 16g

SARDINES WITH MUSTARD
SERVES 1

A sardine is a species of small, oily fish related to a herring. Most sardines found in supermarkets are canned and packed in oil. They have a distinctively fishy flavor, often described as an acquired taste. Although incredibly high in sodium, sardines are an excellent source of Omega-3 fatty acids.

1 large or 2 small smoked sardines (2 ounces)
1 teaspoon Dijon mustard
¼ jalapeño pepper, thinly sliced
1 lemon quarter

■ Place the sardine on a plate and top with the mustard and jalapeño. Serve garnished with the lemon quarter.

NUTRITION FACTS: Calories: 104; Calories from Fat: 51; Fat: 5.7g; Saturated Fat: 0.7g; Cholesterol: 68mg; Sodium: 299mg; Carbohydrates: 0.5g; Dietary Fiber: 0g; Protein: 12.1g

SMOKED SALMON NORI

SERVES 1

Made by curing and smoking a fillet of salmon, smoked salmon has become a breakfast staple across the United States. With its salty fishy flavor, it can be eaten as a filling in omelets or atop a bagel with cream cheese. Although it has a high fat content, smoked salmon is rich in Omega-3 fatty acids. Omega-3s, or "healthy fats," help lower blood pressure and reduce the risk of blood clots. The American Medical Association suggests that a healthy diet include at least one serving of fatty fish (e.g., salmon) per week.

¼ nori sheet
2 teaspoons cream cheese
2 ounces smoked salmon
1 inch English cucumber, thinly sliced
4 watercress leaves

■ Lay the nori on a flat surface and spread with the cream cheese. Top with the salmon, cucumber and watercress leaves and roll into a cylinder. Don't worry if it isn't very neat. Serve as is or cut into 2 to 4 pieces.

NUTRITION FACTS: Calories: 98; Calories from Fat: 43; Fat: 4.8g; Saturated Fat: 2g; Cholesterol: 20mg; Sodium: 1160mg; Carbohydrates: 1.3g; Dietary Fiber: 0g; Protein: 11.6g

SMOKED SALMON "TARTARE"
SERVES 3

first developed this recipe as a topping for crackers but found I liked it so much I always ate it alone. It makes a great snack—even for breakfast!

½ **pound smoked salmon, finely chopped**
¼ **red onion, halved and finely chopped**
2 scallions, finely chopped
3 tablespoons capers, drained
2 tablespoons finely chopped fresh Italian flat-leaf parsley leaves, plus additional for garnish
1 teaspoon fresh lemon juice or red wine vinegar
¼ **to** ½ **teaspoon black pepper**

■ Place all the ingredients in a small bowl and gently mix. Cover and refrigerate for at least 1 hour and up to 6 hours. Serve garnished with the parsley.

NUTRITION FACTS: Calories: 99; Calories from Fat: 31; Fat: 3.4g; Saturated Fat: 0.7g; Cholesterol: 17mg; Sodium: 1770mg; Carbohydrates: 2.4g; Dietary Fiber: 0.8g; Protein: 14.4g

AVOCADO AND SHRIMP "SEVICHE"
SERVES 2

Seviche is classically made with raw scallops, which "cook" in the lime juice. In this recipe, I substituted the scallops with shrimp, which require cooking, making it less seviche-like in method but identical in flavor and ingredients.

¼ **pound cooked shrimp, cut into large chunks**
Juice and freshly grated zest of ½ lime
2 teaspoons chopped fresh cilantro leaves
¼ **perfectly ripe avocado, cubed**
2 tablespoons chopped fresh pineapple
¼ **beefsteak tomato, cored and chopped**
Pinch crushed red pepper flakes
Pinch kosher salt

■ Place all the ingredients in a large glass or ceramic bowl and toss to combine. Cover and refrigerate for at least 20 minutes but no longer than 1 hour.

NUTRITION FACTS: Calories: 104; Calories from Fat: 39; Fat: 4.3g; Saturated Fat: 0.7g; Cholesterol: 111mg; Sodium: 275mg; Carbohydrates: 4.1g; Dietary Fiber: 2g; Protein: 12.5g

GINGER TOFU
SERVES 2

I am not a huge tofu fan but when my pal Sarah Conover called to give me this recipe, I was intrigued. And then I ate the whole thing. And now I always keep tofu in the fridge: it's a great source of protein. Research suggests that soy reduces the risk of prostate cancer.

¼ teaspoon grated fresh ginger
¼ teaspoon grated garlic
1½ teaspoons low-sodium soy sauce
1 teaspoon water
½ teaspoon toasted sesame oil
⅖ of a 1-pound block silken tofu (⅖ pound, 6.4 ounces), cut into cubes
2 scallions, greens only, chopped
1 teaspoon lightly toasted white sesame seeds
2 thin slices fresh ginger (optional)

■ Place the grated ginger, garlic, soy sauce, water and sesame oil in a small bowl and mix well. Add the tofu and gently toss. Serve immediately, garnished with the scallions and sesame seeds, or cover and refrigerate overnight. Serve garnished with the ginger slices, if desired.

NUTRITION FACTS: Calories: 83; Calories from Fat: 39; Fat: 4.4g; Saturated Fat: 0.6g; Cholesterol: 0mg; Sodium: 168mg; Carbohydrates: 4.2g; Dietary Fiber: 0.7; Protein: 7g

SHRIMP COCKTAIL

SERVES 1

A departure from traditional shrimp cocktail, this chunky, creamy, tart-sweet rendition is more flavorful and more interesting.

2 teaspoons mango chutney
1 teaspoon low-fat Greek yogurt
½ teaspoon chopped fresh cilantro leaves
3 ounces cooked and cooled shrimp

■ Place the chutney and yogurt in the corner of a small serving bowl and gently mix. Add the cilantro and top with the shrimp.

NUTRITION FACTS: Calories: 104; Calories from Fat: 9; Fat: 1g; Saturated Fat: 0g; Cholesterol: 166mg; Sodium: 215mg; Carbohydrates: 4.9g; Dietary Fiber: 0g; Protein: 18.2g

TUNA WITH CAPERS, DILL AND LEMON JUICE
SERVES 4

A light, fresh Mediterranean inspired tuna salad without mayo.

1½ cans white tuna in water, drained well
3 tablespoons drained capers
3 tablespoons chopped fresh dill
2½ teaspoons olive oil
2 teaspoons fresh lemon juice
⅛ teaspoon kosher salt
⅛ teaspoon black pepper

■ Place everything in a bowl and mix to combine. Serve immediately or cover and refrigerate up to overnight.

NUTRITION FACTS: Calories: 99; Calories from Fat: 41; Fat: 4.5g; Saturated Fat: 0.8g; Cholesterol: 22mg; Sodium: 295mg; Carbohydrates: 1.9g; Dietary Fiber: 0.6g; Protein: 12.8g

TUNA WITH OLIVE PASTE AND FENNEL

SERVES 3

If you think tuna needs mayo in order to be moist, you are most mistaken: the olive paste supplies plenty of moisture and far more flavor than mayo. And the fennel adds the welcome taste of licorice!

1 can white tuna in water, drained well
½ fennel bulb or English cucumber, chopped
3 tablespoons chopped fresh basil leaves
3 tablespoons chopped red onion
2 celery stalks, finely chopped
1 tablespoon olive paste
1 teaspoon sherry vinegar
¼ teaspoon kosher salt
¼ teaspoon black pepper

■ Place all the ingredients in a small bowl, gently mix, cover and refrigerate for at least 1 hour and up to 4 hours.

NUTRITION FACTS: Calories: 95; Calories from Fat: 28; Fat: 3.1g; Saturated Fat: 0.6g; Cholesterol: 19mg; Sodium: 375mg; Carbohydrates: 5.2g; Dietary Fiber: 2.1g; Protein: 11.7g

TURKEY SLIDERS
SERVES 1

I've often noticed that I crave sugar when what I really need is protein. This little herby burger is a perfect afternoon pick-me-up when I am smart enough to pay attention.

1½ ounces ground turkey or chicken
1 tablespoon chopped scallion
1 tablespoon chopped fresh cilantro leaves
¼ teaspoon freshly grated orange zest
¼ teaspoon curry powder
¼ teaspoon kosher salt
1 lime quarter

■ Place all of the ingredients in a small mixing bowl and, using your hands, gently mix until everything is evenly incorporated. Form into a patty and make a small indentation about the size of a dime in the middle of each side; handle as little as possible: do not work more than necessary.

■ Place a cast iron skillet over high heat and when it is hot but not smoking, add the burger to the dry pan. Cook until well seared on both sides, about 5 minutes. Garnish with the lime quarter.

NUTRITION FACTS: Calories: 104; Calories from Fat: 51; Fat: 5.7g; Saturated Fat: 1.5g; Cholesterol: 43mg; Sodium: 629mg; Carbohydrates: 0.9g; Dietary Fiber: 0g; Protein: 11.8g

CANADIAN BACON WITH BROWN SUGAR AND MUSTARD

SERVES 1

Like traditional bacon, Canadian bacon is salted and cured. However, it is far leaner. It never reaches the same crispiness when cooked but is, instead, meant to be served when still soft and juicy.

3 slices Canadian bacon
1 teaspoon Dijon mustard
½ teaspoon brown sugar
Pinch black pepper (optional)

■ Place a large nonstick skillet over medium heat and when it is hot, add the bacon. Cook until browned, about 1 minute per side. Brush with the mustard and sprinkle with sugar and pepper, if desired.

NUTRITION FACTS: Calories: 99; Calories from Fat: 38; Fat: 4.2g; Saturated Fat: 1.3g; Cholesterol: 29mg; Sodium: 860mg; Carbohydrates: 2.8g; Dietary Fiber: 0.8g; Protein: 12g

BLT

SERVES 1

A true BLT: bacon, lettuce and tomato—no bread.

1 red leaf or romaine lettuce leaf
3 slices turkey bacon, cooked according to package directions
2 slices tomato
$\frac{1}{10}$ avocado, thinly sliced

■ Place the lettuce leaf on a flat surface flatten as much as possible. Top with the bacon slices and then the tomato and avocado. Roll into a cylinder and eat!

NUTRITION FACTS: Calories: 102; Calories from Fat: 41; Fat: 4.6g; Saturated Fat: 0g; Cholesterol: 30mg; Sodium: 425mg; Carbohydrates: 3.8g; Dietary Fiber: 2.3g; Protein: 10g

CURRY-RUBBED CHICKEN TENDERS

SERVES 4

What I love about chicken tenders is that you can buy them by the package and because they are small, they cook quickly and take on a lot of flavor. Generally three chicken tenders equal 100 calories. The rub is calorie free.

2 teaspoons curry powder
½ teaspoon kosher salt
¼ teaspoon chili powder
⅛ teaspoon ground chipotle chili powder
⅛ teaspoon ground cinnamon
8 ounces boneless, skinless chicken tenders

■ To make the rub: place the curry powder, salt, chili powder, chipotle powder and cinnamon in a small bowl and mix well. Dredge the tenders in the rub. Place a nonstick skillet over medium heat and when it is hot, add the tenders. Cook until deeply browned on both sides, 5 to 7 minutes. Serve hot or cold.

NUTRITION FACTS: Calories: 97; Calories from Fat: 20; Fat: 2.2g; Saturated Fat: 0.6g; Cholesterol: 48mg; Sodium: 335mg; Carbohydrates: 0.7; Dietary Fiber: 0g; Protein: 17.7g

BEEF AU POIVRE SLIDERS

SERVES 1

Very peppery little burgers.

- ¼ teaspoon coarsely ground black pepper
- ¼ plus ⅛ teaspoon kosher salt
- ¼ teaspoon dried oregano
- 1⅞ ounces ground beef, formed into a patty
- 1 lemon quarter

■ Place the pepper, salt and oregano on a small plate and mix well. Dredge the patty in the mixture. Make a small indentation about the size of a dime in the middle of each side. Handle as little as possible; do not work more than necessary.

■ Place a cast iron skillet over high heat and when it is hot but not smoking, add the burger to the dry pan. Cook until well seared on both sides, about 5 minutes. Serve with the lemon quarter.

NUTRITION FACTS: Calories: 101; Calories from Fat: 30; Fat: 3.4g; Saturated Fat: 1.3g; Cholesterol: 47mg; Sodium: 35mg; Carbohydrates: 0.6g; Dietary Fiber: 0g; Protein: 16.2g

SMOKED HAM PITA

SERVES 1

You can either cut the pita in half to make two circles or in half to make two little purses. Either way, this is an easy little sandwich to drop in your child's backpack or your bag or briefcase.

½ **reduced-carb pita bread**
1 **teaspoon Dijon mustard**
1 **ounce smoked ham**
½ **leaf romaine lettuce**
2 **thin slices tomato**
1 **thin slice red onion**

■ Place the pita bread on a flat surface and spread with the mustard. Fill with the ham, lettuce, tomato and onion.

NUTRITION FACTS: Calories: 100; Calories from Fat: 23; Fat: 2.5g; Saturated Fat: 0.8g; Cholesterol: 14mg; Sodium: 478mg; Carbohydrates: 12.8g; Dietary Fiber: 1g; Protein: 6.1g

TOMATO WRAPPED WITH VIRGINIA HAM AND SPICY MUSTARD

SERVES 1

This isn't the kind of thing to eat on a first date: it's very messy and has the potential to fall apart—but it hits the spot when you want a hit of protein. Think of it as a sandwich with the ham as the bread and the tomato as the filling.

1.75 ounces smoked ham
1 teaspoon spicy mustard
2 slices tomato

■ Place the ham on a flat surface and spread with the mustard. Top with the tomato. Roll into a cylinder and eat!

NUTRITION FACTS: Calories: 102; Calories from Fat: 47; Fat: 5.3g; Saturated Fat: 1.5g; Cholesterol: 28mg; Sodium: 649mg; Carbohydrates: 4.2g; Dietary Fiber: 1.5g; Protein: 9.3g

FRUIT DESSERTS

MANGO WITH LIME AND RED PEPPER FLAKES
SERVES 1

Considered by many to be a tropical fruit, mangoes are actually native to Southeast Asia. Sweet and juicy, mangoes are high in beta-carotene, which helps improve eyesight. When selecting a mango at the grocery store, be sure to choose a firm, plump one that gives slightly with applied pressure.

¾ cup diced mango
Juice of ½ lime
¼ teaspoon crushed red pepper flakes
1 lime quarter

■ Place the mango in a bowl, add the lime juice and red pepper flakes, and gently stir. Serve garnished with the lime quarter.

NUTRITION FACTS: Calories: 95; Calories from Fat: 4; Fat: 0.4g; Saturated Fat: 0g; Cholesterol: 0mg; Sodium: 3mg; Carbohydrates: 25g; Dietary Fiber: 2.6g; Protein: 0.8g

GRILLED PINEAPPLE
SERVES 4

I understand that few people would want to fire up a grill just for one pineapple. So next time you are grilling, throw a pineapple on and either serve it for dessert or save it for snacking: the pineapple is equally good cold and hot.

1 tablespoon unsalted butter, melted
1 tablespoon brown sugar
Juice of ½ lime
1 fresh pineapple, cored and cut into eighths lengthwise

■ Place the butter, brown sugar and lime juice in a small bowl and mix well.
■ Prepare a grill. Brush the butter mixture on the pineapple, place on the grill and cook, turning once, until lightly browned on both sides, about 4 minutes. Drizzle with the remaining butter mixture and serve immediately.

NUTRITION FACTS: Calories: 102; Calories from Fat: 27; Fat: 3g; Saturated Fat: 1.8g; Cholesterol: 8mg; Sodium: 22mg; Carbohydrates: 20.1g; Dietary Fiber: 1.9g; Protein: 0.8g

MAPLE-ROASTED PEARS

SERVES 4

Poaching is the most common cooking method for pears, but I prefer the results of roasting: deep, rich and creamy sweet.

2 firm pears, peeled, quartered lengthwise and cored
2 tablespoons plus 2 teaspoons real maple syrup
2 teaspoons freshly squeezed lemon juice
½ teaspoon vanilla extract
Pinch ground cinnamon
Pinch kosher salt

■ Preheat the oven to 400°F. Place all of the ingredients in a bowl and toss well. Place the pears in a small baking pan and drizzle with the remaining liquid from the bowl. Transfer to the oven and roast until deep brown and tender, 30 minutes. Serve at any temperature.

NUTRITION FACTS: Calories: 98; Calories from Fat: 1: Fat: 0.2g; Saturated Fat: 0g; Cholesterol: 0mg; Sodium: 41mg; Carbohydrates: 25.4g; Dietary Fiber: 3.3g; Protein: 0.4g

BAKED GRAPEFRUIT WITH MINT AND HONEY

SERVES 2

My daughter Lauren is a grapefruit fanatic, often eating four or five a day during the winter, so it's often hard for me to get my hands on any grapefruits. When I am able, this is my most beloved recipe.

1 large grapefruit, halved
½ tablespoon honey or brown sugar
Mint leaves

■ Prepare the broiler. Place the grapefruit, cut side up, on a large baking sheet. Drizzle with the honey and transfer to the broiler. Broil until the top is browned and bubbling, about 5 minutes. Set aside for 3 to 4 minutes and serve warm, garnished with mint leaves.

NUTRITION FACTS: Calories: 69; Calories from Fat: 1; Fat: 0.2g; Cholesterol: 0mg; Sodium: 0mg; Carbohydrates: 17.7g; Dietary Fiber: 1.8g; Protein: 1.1g

STRAWBERRIES WITH BALSAMIC VINEGAR AND BLACK PEPPER

SERVES 2

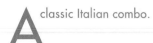A classic Italian combo.

½ cup balsamic vinegar
1½ pints strawberries, stems left on
1 teaspoon coarsely cracked black pepper

■ Place the balsamic vinegar in a small pot and bring to a boil over high heat. Reduce the heat to medium and simmer until it is about one-third of its volume, about 5 minutes. (When you take it off the stove it will continue reducing, so use it quickly before it disappears.)
■ Drizzle the warm balsamic vinegar over the strawberries and sprinkle with the black pepper. Serve immediately.

NUTRITION FACTS: Calories: 101; Calories from Fat: 8; Fat: 0.8g; Saturated Fat: 0g; Cholesterol: 0mg; Sodium: 6mg; Carbohydrates: 21.8g; Dietary Fiber: 5.6g; Protein: 1.9g

APPLEBANANASAUCE

SERVES 4, ABOUT ¾ CUP PER SERVING

I developed this scrumptious snack for my children when they were younger—although it's now a favorite of mine—because I had a lot of over-ripe bananas. Now I buy bananas for the sole purpose of ripening them in order to make Applebananasauce.

3 tart apples, cored, peeled and sliced
3 small over-ripe bananas, cut into quarters
1 teaspoon ground cinnamon

Place the apples in the bowl of a food processor fitted with a steel blade and process until well chopped. Scrape down the sides of the bowl and add the bananas and cinnamon. Process until smooth. Transfer to a bowl, cover and refrigerate for at least 1 hour and up to 2 days.

NUTRITION FACTS: Calories: 100; Calories from Fat: 3; Fat: 0.4g; Saturated Fat: 0g; Cholesterol: 0mg; Sodium: 2mg; Carbohydrates: 26.3g; Dietary Fiber: 4.1g; Protein: 0.8g

FRUIT KABOBS

SERVES 1

E specially refreshing in the summer, but great year-round.

⅓ **large banana, sliced**
1 kiwi, sliced
5 strawberries, left whole if small or halved if large
Mint leaves (optional)

■ Thread the fruit on a skewer. Serve garnished with the mint leaves, if desired.

NUTRITION FACTS: Calories: 101; Calories from Fat: 6; Fat: 0.7g; Saturated Fat: 0g; Cholesterol: 0mg; Sodium: 3mg; Carbohydrates: 24.7g; Dietary Fiber: 4.5g; Protein: 1.7g

TEA-POACHED PRUNES

SERVES 4

Made from dried plums, prunes are naturally sweet with a sticky chewy texture. When you poach them, they become mellow and meltingly soft. Just like plums, prunes are rich in phenols, an antioxidant known for its prevention of heart-related diseases. Additionally, prunes are an excellent source of vitamin A.

20 pitted prunes
2 bags black tea
2 bags green tea
½ lemon, thinly sliced
Freshly grated zest of ½ lemon, or more to taste

■ Place everything in a small bowl or cup and add boiling water to cover. Let steep 10 minutes, remove tea bags and let sit at least 2 hours. Cover and refrigerate for up to 1 month.

NUTRITION FACTS: Calories: 101; Calories from Fat: 1; Fat: 0.2g; Saturated Fat: 0g; Cholesterol: 0mg; Sodium: 1mg; Carbohydrates: 26.8g; Dietary Fiber: 3g; Protein: 0.9g

CHUNKY CRANBERRY APPLESAUCE
SERVES 2

A rosy, chunky applesauce made richer, tarter and more beautiful by the addition of cranberries.

2 Granny Smith or other tart apples, peeled, if desired, and cut in small dice
⅓ cup fresh or frozen cranberries
2 tablespoons water
1 tablespoon sugar

■ Place all of the ingredients in a saucepan, cover and cook over medium-low heat until the apples are tender, about 30 minutes. Coarsely mash (using a potato masher or fork) and set aside to cool. Serve warm or refrigerate until cold.

NUTRITION FACTS: Calories: 103; Calories from Fat: 2; Fat: 0.3g; Saturated Fat: 0g; Cholesterol: 0mg; Sodium: 2mg; Carbohydrates: 27.3g; Dietary Fiber: 4g; Protein: 0.4g

FIGS AND RASPBERRIES

SERVES 1

A simple, elegant and delicious dessert. Fresh figs are high in potassium (about twice that of bananas) and help lower blood pressure.

2 fresh figs, quartered
10 fresh raspberries
1 teaspoon honey
½ teaspoon unsweetened cocoa powder
1 tablespoon Greek yogurt

■ Place the figs and raspberries in a shallow bowl and drizzle with the honey. Sprinkle with the cocoa powder and serve topped with the yogurt or with the yogurt on the side for dipping.

NUTRITION FACTS: Calories: 101; Calories from Fat: 7; Fat: 0.7g; Saturated Fat: 0g; Cholesterol: 1mg; Sodium: 6mg; Carbohydrates: 24.4g; Dietary Fiber: 3.8g; Protein: 2.2g

BERRY RHUBARB COMPOTE
SERVES 4

I f I only had one dessert to eat for the rest of my life, this would be it! To me, there is no better combination than tart rhubarb with berries. If you prefer one berry over all others, simply substitute it.

3 cups chopped rhubarb
1 cup blueberries
2 cups strawberries
1½ cups raspberries
1 teaspoon cornstarch
1 tablespoon sugar

Place the rhubarb, berries and cornstarch in a medium saucepan and cook over medium heat until it reaches a low boil, about 7 minutes. Reduce the heat to low and cook until the rhubarb is soft and the mixture has thickened, about 30 minutes. Off the heat, add the sugar and stir until it has dissolved. Serve warm or at room temperature.

NUTRITION FACTS: Calories: 102; Calories from Fat: 7; Fat: 0.8g; Saturated Fat: 0g; Cholesterol: 0mg; Sodium: 5mg; Carbohydrates: 24.2g; Dietary Fiber: 7g; Protein: 2.1g

GINGER-ROASTED PEARS
SERVES 2

I love the crisp texture of just slightly under-ripe pears, but I also love how roasting transforms them: it renders them softer and more buttery and removes the cloying sweetness that I hate in ripe pears.

Pears are very high in antioxidants (and get higher as they ripen) and in dietary fiber, vitamin C, copper and vitamin K.

- **4 firm, not quite ripe yet brown pears**
- **½ cup white wine**
- **½ cup water**
- **4 quarter-size slices fresh gingerroot**
- **2 tablespoons brown sugar**

■ Preheat the oven to 425°F. Place the pears as snugly as possible in a small pan or ovenproof skillet. Pour the wine and water in the bottom, add the ginger and brown sugar and stir to combine. Transfer to the oven and roast until the pears are tender and just starting to bubble, about 1 hour. Spoon the sauce from the bottom of the pan on top of the pears and serve warm.

NUTRITION FACTS: Calories: 102; Calories from Fat: 1; Fat: 0.1g; Saturated Fat: 0g; Cholesterol: 0mg; Sodium: 4mg; Carbohydrates: 21.4g; Dietary Fiber: 3.2g; Protein: 0.4g

POACHED PEACHES

SERVES 4

Peaches are rarely found poached—poaching is usually reserved for pears—but these gently vanilla-flavored peaches are lovely for a late-night dessert.

½ **cup dry white wine**
½ **cup water**
3 **tablespoons sugar**
1 **vanilla bean, split lengthwise**
4 **firm but ripe peaches, halved or cut into thick slices**

■ Place the wine, water, sugar and vanilla bean in a medium-size saucepan and bring to a boil over high heat. Reduce the heat and simmer until the sugar has dissolved, about 3 minutes. Off the heat, remove the vanilla bean and scrape the seeds back into the syrup. Return to a low boil. Add the peaches and simmer until tender, 10 minutes. Transfer to a bowl, cover and refrigerate for at least 2 hours and up to overnight.

NUTRITION FACTS: Calories: 99; Calories from Fat: 2; Fat: 0.2g; Saturated Fat: 0g; Cholesterol: 0mg; Sodium: 2mg; Carbohydrates: 19.6g; Dietary Fiber: 1.5g; Protein: 0.9g

PEACHES 'N' CREAM
SERVES 1

This compote-like dish tastes just like the inside of a cobbler or crisp.

1 perfectly ripe peach, sliced
1½ tablespoons heavy cream
⅛ teaspoon ground ginger
Pinch kosher salt
6 blueberries

■ Preheat the oven to 500°F. Place the peach slices in a small pan, transfer to the oven, and cook until they brown and bubble, about 10 minutes.

■ Place the cream, ginger and salt in a small bowl and stir well. Off heat, pour the mixture over the hot peaches. Garnish with the blueberries and serve warm.

NUTRITION FACTS: Calories: 91; Calories from Fat: 52; Fat: 5.8g; Saturated Fat: 3.5g; Cholesterol: 21mg; Sodium: 161mg; Carbohydrates: 9.9g; Dietary Fiber: 1.5g; Protein: 1.2g

FROZEN DESSERTS

BANANA PEACH "SORBET"

SERVES 4, ABOUT ¾ CUP PER SERVING

The most popular fruit in the U.S., bananas are ever-present in most households. If your house is like mine, the window for banana perfection is small and over-ripe bananas are readily available. My suggestion is that you keep a few sliced bananas (as well as berries) in your freezer so you can make this easy, fast dessert anytime.

Substitute the peaches with mangoes, papaya, or any kind of berry.

2 over-ripe bananas, thinly sliced and frozen
2 cups chopped fresh peaches, peeled, if desired, and frozen
½ teaspoon vanilla extract
⅓ cup plain low-fat yogurt

■ Place the frozen bananas and peaches in the bowl of a food processor fitted with a steel blade. Process until smooth. Add the vanilla and yogurt and process until completely incorporated. Serve immediately or cover and freeze in individual portions for up to 2 weeks. If you freeze portions, let them sit at room temperature for 10 minutes before eating.

NUTRITION FACTS: Calories: 100; Calories from Fat: 7; Fat: 0.7g; Saturated Fat: 0g; Cholesterol: 1mg; Sodium: 15mg; Carbohydrates: 23.1g; Dietary Fiber: 2.8g; Protein: 2.5g

PINK GRAPEFRUIT GRANITA
SERVES 4

It's hard to imagine that merely freezing and stirring grapefruit juice can so fully transform it into a frozen delight. It's great as a dessert or palate cleanser. Grapefruit is a particularly good fruit for a granita: highly acidic with a tangy flavor, it has an underlying sweetness that the small amount of sugar releases. Just like oranges, grapefruit are an excellent source of vitamin C.

3 cups fresh pink grapefruit juice
3½ tablespoons sugar
1 tablespoon finely chopped fresh mint leaves

■ Place the juice and sugar in a shallow pan and mix until the sugar has dissolved. Transfer to the freezer. Using a fork, stir every 15 minutes until frozen, about 2 hours. After 2 hours, serve or cover and freeze in individual portions for up to 2 weeks. Garnish with the mint leaves.

NUTRITION FACTS: Calories: 98; Calories from Fat: 2; Fat: 0.2g; Saturated Fat: 0g; Cholesterol: 0mg; Sodium: 0mg; Carbohydrates: 25g; Dietary Fiber: 1.9g; Protein: 1.1g

CAPPUCCINO GRANITA
SERVES 2

I t wasn't until I made this wonderful strong, grainy granita—an Italian semifrozen dessert—that I appreciated putting a little bit of sugar in coffee. If you like cocoa powder sprinkled on your cappuccino you can add it here too.

2 cups just-brewed espresso or strong coffee (caffeinated or decaf)
⅔ cup whole milk
1 tablespoon sugar
½ teaspoon ground cinnamon
1 tablespoon heavy cream
6 coffee beans (optional)

■ Place the coffee, milk, sugar and cinnamon in a cup and mix until the sugar has dissolved. Set aside until it reaches room temperature. Pour into a shallow pan and transfer to the freezer. Using a fork, stir every 15 minutes until frozen, about 2 hours. After 2 hours, serve or cover and freeze in individual portions for up to 2 weeks. Garnish with the heavy cream and, if desired, coffee beans.

NUTRITION FACTS: Calories: 99; Calories from Fat: 49; Fat: 5.4g; Saturated Fat: 3.2g; Cholesterol: 1.8mg; Sodium: 35mg; Carbohydrates: 10.2g; Dietary Fiber: 0g; Protein: 2.8g

RASPBERRY BANANA "SORBET"
SERVES 4

Be sure to use frozen raspberries and bananas because the texture of this sweet, smooth and tart sorbet is best when just made. If you use fruit that isn't frozen you will have to freeze it and then process it again for the best consistency. The sharp deep pink of it is absolutely enticing.

2 cups frozen fresh raspberries
1½ over-ripe bananas, sliced and frozen
¾ cup plain low-fat yogurt
2 teaspoons fresh lemon juice (optional)

▨ Place the raspberries in a food processor fitted with a steel blade and pulse until finely chopped. Scrape down the sides. Add the bananas and pulse until smooth. Scrape down the sides. Add the yogurt and lemon juice, if desired, and pulse until completely incorporated and bright pink. Serve immediately or cover and freeze in individual portions for up to 2 weeks. If you freeze portions, let them sit at room temperature for 10 minutes before eating.

NUTRITION FACTS: Calories: 101; Calories from Fat: 11; Fat: 1.3g; Saturated Fat: 0.5g; Cholesterol: 3mg; Sodium: 33mg; Carbohydrates: 20.9g; Dietary Fiber: 5.2g; Protein: 3.6g

PINEAPPLE FRO-YO

SERVES 4

The combination of the lush banana and juicy, sweet-tart pineapple is reminiscent of the tropics. For even more tropical flavor, substitute 3 tablespoons lite coconut milk and 2 tablespoons water for the yogurt. The pineapple core holds much of its nutrients so be sure you add a little into the mix.

1½ over-ripe bananas, frozen and sliced
2 cups frozen pineapple chunks
½ cup plain low-fat yogurt
1 teaspoon freshly grated lime zest

■ Place the frozen banana and pineapple chunks in the bowl of a food processor fitted with a steel blade. Process until smooth. Gradually add the yogurt and lime zest and process until completely incorporated. Serve immediately or cover and freeze in individual portions for up to 2 weeks. If you freeze portions, let them sit at room temperature for 10 minutes before eating.

NUTRITION FACTS: Calories: 98; Calories from Fat: 6; Fat: 0.7g; Saturated Fat: 0g; Cholesterol: 2mg; Sodium: 23mg; Carbohydrates: 22.5g; Dietary Fiber: 2.3g; Protein: 2.5g

BERRY FRO-YO

SERVES 4

Although berries are among the leading sources of fiber and very high in antioxidants, you'll eat this because it's so refreshing and delicious.

2½ cups strawberries, sliced and frozen
2 cups blueberries, frozen
½ cup plus 2 tablespoons plain low-fat yogurt
1 teaspoon fresh lemon juice

■ Place the frozen berries in the bowl of a food processor fitted with a steel blade. Process until smooth. Gradually add the yogurt and lemon juice and process until completely incorporated. Serve immediately or cover and freeze in individual portions for up to 2 weeks. If you freeze portions, let them sit at room temperature for 10 minutes before eating.

NUTRITION FACTS: Calories: 95; Calories from Fat: 10; Fat: 1.1g; Saturated Fat: 0g; Cholesterol: 2mg; Sodium: 28mg; Carbohydrates: 20.2g; Dietary Fiber: 3.5g; Protein: 3.2g

COOKIES, BROWNIES AND THAT SORT OF THING

BROWNIES

MAKES 45 BROWNIES, 1 BROWNIE PER SERVING

U nlike most brownies, these are at their peak after they have cooled to room temperature and then refrigerated. Honestly, it's worth the wait!

½ pound (2 sticks) unsalted butter
½ pound semisweet chocolate
3 ounces unsweetened chocolate
3 large eggs, at room temperature
1 tablespoon vanilla extract
1 cup sugar
¾ cup all purpose flour
1½ teaspoons baking powder
½ teaspoon kosher salt

▓ Preheat the oven to 350°F. Line a 9 x 13-inch baking pan with parchment paper.
▓ Place the butter in a saucepan over medium heat and when it starts to melt, reduce the heat to low and add the chocolates. Cook over the lowest possible heat, stirring all the while, until everything is melted, 3 to 5 minutes. Set aside to cool.
▓ Place the eggs, vanilla and sugar in a large mixing bowl and stir until just combined. Add the chocolate mixture and stir until just combined. Add the flour, baking powder and salt and stir until just combined. Pour into the prepared pan, transfer to the oven, and bake until your kitchen smells like chocolate and a toothpick inserted comes out clean, 30 to 35 minutes. Set aside to cool to room temperature. Cover and refrigerate overnight. Cut into 45 brownies. Wrap individually in plastic wrap and freeze for up to 2 months.

NUTRITION FACTS: Calories: 105; Calories from Fat: 64; Fat: 7.1g; Saturated Fat: 4.5g; Cholesterol: 27mg; Sodium: 66mg; Carbohydrates: 10g; Dietary Fiber: 0.6g; Protein: 1.3g

RICE CRISPY TREATS

MAKES 8 TREATS, 1 TREAT PER SERVING

A perfect, surprisingly low-calorie, low-fat treat for a kid, or for when you feel like a kid.

1 teaspoon unsalted butter
¼ pound marshmallows
¾ teaspoon kosher salt
3 cups puffed-rice cereal such as Rice Krispies
Unsweetened cocoa powder (optional)

■ Line an 8 x 8-inch pan with parchment paper.
■ Place the butter in a small pan and cook over low heat until melted. Add the marshmallows and cook until melted. Add the salt and cereal and mix well. Quickly transfer to the prepared pan and pat down. Set aside to cool. Divide into 8 pieces. Dust with cocoa powder, if desired. Transfer to a container and store at room temperature for up to 1 week.

NUTRITION FACTS: Calories: 91; Calories from Fat: 6; Fat: 0.6g; Saturated Fat: 0g; Cholesterol: 1mg; Sodium: 328mg; Carbohydrates: 20.1g; Dietary Fiber: 0g; Protein: 0.8g

CHOCOLATE CEREAL BITES
SERVES 2

S ounds strange, tastes great. You can alter the cereal but just remember to keep an eye on the calorie count.

⅓ **cup semisweet chocolate chips**
¾ **cup plus 2 tablespoons Rice Chex cereal**

■ Line a plate with parchment or wax paper.
■ Place the chocolate chips in a small bowl and microwave until melted. Add the Chex and mix until coated. Divide the mixture into 6 pieces and place on the prepared plate. Set aside or refrigerate until completely hardened.

NUTRITION FACTS: Calories: 95; Calories from Fat: 26; Fat: 2.8g; Saturated Fat: 1.4g; Cholesterol: 0mg; Sodium: 101mg; Carbohydrates: 15.9g; Dietary Fiber: 0.8g; Protein: 1.4g

SALTED CARAMELS

MAKES 32 CANDIES, 1 CANDY PER SERVING

With a Starbucks down the street from my home, my children often tagged along on my many trips. My son Ben, not ready for coffee, always asked for caramels which sort of horrified me, as I assumed they were chock-full of junk. It turns out they aren't; in fact, you get lots of flavor without too many calories.

- **2 cups sugar**
- **½ cup corn syrup**
- **½ cup water**
- **2 cups heavy cream**
- **5 tablespoons unsalted butter**
- **1 teaspoon kosher salt**
- **1 teaspoon sea salt, or herb-flavored salt**

▨ Line an 8 x 8-inch baking pan with parchment paper.
▨ Place the sugar, corn syrup and water in a heavy saucepan and bring to a boil, stirring until the sugar is dissolved. Continue boiling, without stirring, until golden brown, about 5 minutes.
▨ Meanwhile, place the cream, butter and salt in a small saucepan and bring to a boil over medium heat.
▨ Gradually add the cream mixture to the sugar mixture and cook over medium-low heat, without stirring, until a thermometer registers 245° to 248°F, when the bubbles have bubbles. Pour into the prepared pan and set aside until completely cooled, about 2 hours. Cut into 32 pieces and, if desired, wrap each piece in wax paper, twisting the ends like saltwater taffies. Refrigerate for up to 2 weeks.

NUTRITION FACTS: Calories: 104; Calories from Fat: 41; Fat: 4.6g; Saturated Fat: 2.9g; Cholesterol: 15mg; Sodium: 89mg; Carbohydrates: 16.4g; Dietary Fiber: 0g; Protein: 0.2g

COCOA MERINGUE COOKIES
MAKES ABOUT 25 COOKIES, 5 COOKIES PER SERVING

 A light, melt-in-your-mouth exterior with a slightly chewy interior. These cookies are not too sweet but satisfy when you want a little bit of dessert.

2 large egg whites, at room temperature
½ cup sugar
2 teaspoons unsweetened cocoa powder
½ teaspoon vanilla extract
½ teaspoon ground cinnamon
⅛ teaspoon kosher salt
⅛ teaspoon cream of tartar

■ Preheat the oven to 300°F. Line a baking sheet with parchment paper.
■ Place the egg whites in the bowl of a mixer fitted with the whisk attachment and beat until soft peaks form. Gradually add the sugar, cocoa powder, vanilla, cinnamon, salt and cream of tartar.
■ Drop by rounded spoonfuls onto the prepared baking sheet and transfer to the oven. Bake until firm and dry, about 25 minutes. Transfer the baking sheet to a wire cooling rack. Let the sheet cool completely between batches and repeat with the remaining dough.

NUTRITION FACTS: Calories: 87; Calories from Fat: 1; Fat: 0.1g; Saturated Fat: 0g; Cholesterol: 0mg; Sodium: 80mg; Carbohydrates: 20.8g; Dietary Fiber: 0g; Protein: 1.6g

PEANUT BUTTER AND JELLY RICE TREATS

SERVES 1

This combination of two childhood classics is a dream come true!

½ **Rice Crispy Treat (see page 213)**
1 **teaspoon peanut butter**
1 **teaspoon raspberry jam**

■ Split the Rice Crispy Treat into 2 slices. Spread the peanut butter on one slice and top with the raspberry jam. Top with other slice of the Rice Crispy Treat.

NUTRITION FACTS: Calories: 93; Calories from Fat: 27; Fat: 3g; Saturated Fat: 0.7g; Cholesterol: 1mg; Sodium: 188mg; Carbohydrates: 15.5g; Dietary Fiber: 0g; Protein: 1.8g

CHOCOLATE TRUFFLES
MAKES 12 TRUFFLES, 2 TRUFFLES PER SERVING

⅓ **cup semisweet chocolate chips**
½ **cup heavy cream**
1 tablespoon unsweetened cocoa powder

■ Place the chocolate chips in the microwave and heat until melted. Slowly add the cream and mix until well combined. Set aside to cool. When the chocolate is set, divide into 12 small pieces and form into balls. With very cold hands, roll the balls in the cocoa powder. Cover and refrigerate for at least 1 hour and up to 2 days.

NUTRITION FACTS: Calories: 96; Calories from Fat: 64; Fat: 7.1g; Saturated Fat: 4.7g; Cholesterol: 16mg; Sodium: 13mg; Carbohydrates: 7.4g; Dietary Fiber: 0.7g; Protein: 1.2g

COCOA COOKIES

MAKES 36 COOKIES, 1 COOKIE PER SERVING

It's no small feat to eat just one of these rich, deep brown cookies, so if you are someone who has trouble resisting, I suggest you roll the dough into a log and bake only one cookie at a time. You can also bake the whole batch and freeze the cookies after they've cooled; of course, it depends if you can stop yourself from eating too many.

¼ **pound (1 stick) unsalted butter, at room temperature**
½ **cup sugar**
1 **large egg, at room temperature**
1 **teaspoon vanilla extract**
¾ **cup all purpose flour**
¼ **cup graham flour**
½ **cup unsweetened cocoa powder**
½ **teaspoon baking soda**
¼ **teaspoon baking powder**
¼ **teaspoon kosher salt**

▓ Place the butter and sugar in the bowl of a mixer fitted with a paddle attachment and mix until smooth and creamy. Scrape down the sides of the bowl, add the egg, and mix. Scrape down the sides of the bowl, add the remaining ingredients, and mix until everything is well incorporated. Scrape down the sides of the bowl and mix again.
▓ Form the dough into a log and place on a large piece of parchment or wax paper. Fold up the sides of the paper so as to completely envelop the dough. Refrigerate for at least 2 hours and up to 1 week. When ready to use, divide the dough lengthwise into 4 quarters. Divide each quarter into 9 pieces.
▓ Preheat the oven to 350°F. Line a baking sheet with parchment paper. Place 1 cookie or several cookies on the prepared baking sheet and bake until the edges begin to firm up, 12 to 14 minutes. Set aside to cool. Transfer to a container and freeze for up to 2 months.

NUTRITION FACTS: Calories: 51; Calories from Fat: 26; Fat: 2.9g; Saturated Fat: 1.8g; Cholesterol: 13mg; Sodium: 54mg; Carbohydrates: 6.1g; Dietary Fiber: 0.6g; Protein:0.8g

LACY OATMEAL COOKIES
MAKES ABOUT 3 DOZEN COOKIES, 2 COOKIES PER SERVING

Indescribably delicious, delicate and crunchy.

- ¼ pound (1 stick) unsalted butter, at room temperature
- ⅔ cup light brown sugar
- 2 tablespoons water
- 1 teaspoon vanilla extract
- ¼ cup all purpose white flour
- 1¼ cups quick cooking or old fashioned oats

■ Place the butter and sugar in the bowl of a mixer fitted with a paddle attachment and mix until smooth and creamy. Scrape down the sides of the bowl, add the water and vanilla and mix well. Scrape down the sides of the bowl, add the remaining ingredients, and mix until everything is well incorporated. Scrape down the sides of the bowl and mix again.

■ Divide the dough into 36 portions. Cover and refrigerate for up to 2 months or bake.

■ Preheat the oven to 350°F. Line a baking sheet with parchment paper. Drop portions of dough about 2 inches apart on the prepared baking sheet. Transfer to the oven and bake until the cookies begin to brown at the edges and are still soft in the middle, 10 to 12 minutes. Be sure to immediately move the cookies around on the parchment as soon as they come out of the oven or they will stick. Cool on the parchment on the baking sheet. Transfer to a wire rack and repeat with the remaining dough. When fully cooled, place in a container or zipper freezer bag and freeze up to 2 months.

NUTRITION FACTS: Calories: 94; Calories from Fat: 50; Fat: 5.5g; Saturated Fat: 3.3g: Cholesterol: 14mg; Sodium: 38mg; Carbohydrates: 10.5g; Dietary Fiber: 0.6g; Protein: 1g

ALMOST S'MORE

SERVES 1

You can use any kind of graham cracker for this childhood summer indulgence—chocolate and cinnamon graham crackers are awesome options!

1 regular-size marshmallow
1 graham cracker, split in half

■ Place the marshmallow on 1 of the cracker halves and place in the microwave. In my microwave it takes 10 to 15 seconds to puff up and "melt." Remove from the microwave and top with the other graham cracker half.

NUTRITION FACTS: Calories: 98; Calories from Fat: 7; Fat: 0.8g; Saturated Fat: 0g; Cholesterol: 0mg; Sodium: 59mg; Carbohydrates: 22.2g; Dietary Fiber: 0g; Protein: 0.7g

CHOCOLATE CHIP COOKIES

MAKES 48 COOKIES, 2 COOKIES PER SERVING

The classic cookie made with whole wheat graham flour and oats.

¼ pound (1 stick) unsalted butter, at room temperature
¾ cup light brown sugar
1 large egg
1 teaspoon vanilla extract
½ cup rolled oats
1 cup graham flour
½ teaspoon baking soda
½ teaspoon baking powder
½ teaspoon kosher salt
1½ cups semisweet chocolate chips

■ Place the butter and sugar in the bowl of a mixer fitted with the paddle attachment and mix until smooth and creamy. Scrape down the sides of the bowl, add the egg and vanilla, and mix well. Scrape down the sides of the bowl, add the remaining ingredients, and mix until everything is well incorporated. Scrape down the sides of the bowl and mix again.

NUTRITION FACTS: Calories: 98; Calories from Fat: 48; Fat: 5.3g; Saturated Fat: 3g; Cholesterol: 19mg; Sodium: 109mg; Carbohydrates: 11.9g; Dietary Fiber: 0.9g; Protein: 1.3g

■ Form the dough into a log and place on a large piece of parchment or wax paper. Fold up the sides of the paper so as to completely envelop the dough. Refrigerate for at least 2 hours and up to 1 week. When ready to use, divide the dough lengthwise into 4 quarters. Divide each quarter into 12 pieces.
■ Preheat the oven to 350°F. Line a baking sheet with parchment paper. Place 1 cookie or several cookies on the prepared baking sheet and bake until the edges begin to firm up, 12 to 14 minutes. Set aside to cool. Transfer to a container and freeze for up to 2 months.

LEMON MERINGUE COOKIES
MAKES 16 COOKIES, 4 COOKIES PER SERVING

Light, tart and airy, these lovely little cookies are addictive.

2 large egg whites, at room temperature
½ cup sugar
2 teaspoons lemon juice
½ teaspoon freshly grated lemon zest
⅛ teaspoon kosher salt
⅛ teaspoon cream of tartar

▪ Preheat the oven to 300°F. Line a baking sheet with parchment paper.
▪ Place the egg whites in the bowl of a mixer fitted with a whisk attachment and beat until soft peaks form. Gradually add the sugar, lemon juice and zest, salt and cream of tartar.
▪ Drop by rounded spoonfuls onto the prepared baking sheet and transfer to the oven. Bake until firm and dry, about 25 minutes. Transfer the baking sheet to a wire cooling rack. Let the sheet cool completely between batches and repeat with the remaining dough.

NUTRITION FACTS: Calories: 98; Calories from Fat: 0; Fat: 0g; Saturated Fat: 0g; Cholesterol: 0mg; Sodium: 100mg; Carbohydrates: 23.4g; Dietary Fiber: 0g; Protein: 1.8g

PECAN OATMEAL CRISPS

MAKES 20 COOKIES, 2 COOKIES PER SERVING

Like a very nutty, almost-flat oatmeal cookie, these crispy cookies are a great treat paired with coffee or tea.

½ cup lightly toasted pecans
½ cup rolled oats
½ cup light brown sugar
2 tablespoons all purpose flour
⅛ teaspoon baking powder
⅛ teaspoon kosher salt
1 large egg

■ Place the pecans and oats in a food processor fitted with a steel blade and pulse until well chopped but not butter smooth. Add the sugar, flour, baking powder and salt and pulse again. Add the egg and pulse until it becomes a gooey batter. Cover and refrigerate for at least 1 hour.
■ Divide into 20 portions, using teaspoons. Cover and refrigerate for up to 2 months or bake.
■ Preheat the oven to 350°F. Line a baking sheet with parchment paper. Using the amount of cookie dough you want to bake, drop portions of dough on the pan and press them down. Transfer to the oven and bake until lightly colored on the edges, about 12 minutes. Do not remove from the baking sheet until fully cooled.

NUTRITION FACTS: Calories: 93; Calories from Fat: 42; Fat: 4.7g; Saturated Fat: 0.5g; Cholesterol: 21mg; Sodium: 38mg; Carbohydrates: 11.9g; Dietary Fiber: 1g; Protein: 1.8g

BEVERAGES

VIRGIN MARY

SERVES 2

Spicy, smooth and filling, the Virgin Mary is the nonalcoholic offspring of the Bloody Mary, originally simply a mix of tomato juice and vodka. Lore says it later morphed into what it is today when Pete Petitot, its creator, came to New York. Apparently New Yorkers were looking for a little more spice.

The ancient Romans believed that hanging a celery stick around your neck warded off hangovers: perhaps this is how celery sticks got into Bloody Marys.

4 cups low-sodium tomato or V8 juice
2½ tablespoons prepared horseradish, or more to taste
2¼ teaspoons Worcestershire sauce
½ tablespoon Tabasco sauce, or more to taste
1 teaspoon freshly cracked black pepper
2 celery sticks, for stirring
2 lemon slices

■ Place the juice, horseradish, Worcestershire sauce, Tabasco and pepper in a large pitcher and stir well. Garnish with a celery stick and lemon or lime slices.

NUTRITION FACTS: Calories: 105; Calories from Fat: 4; Fat: 0.5g; Saturated Fat: 0g; Cholesterol: 0mg; Sodium: 210 mg; Carbohydrates: 25.7g; Dietary Fiber: 3.3g; Protein: 4.2g

ROOT BEER "FLOAT"

SERVES 1

My friend Susan Orlean swears that the best part of a root beer float—also known as a Black Cow—is when the ice cream melts. So she figured she didn't really need the ice cream and substituted milk. Refreshing and filling, this root beer float is one of her favorite afternoon snacks.

1 can (12 ounces) diet root beer
⅓ cup skim milk

■ Fill a tall glass with the root beer. Slowly add the milk, tipping the glass to the side if it starts to foam too much. Grab a straw and enjoy!

NUTRITION FACTS: Calories: 28; Calories from Fat: 1; Fat: 0.1g; Saturated Fat: 0g; Cholesterol: 2mg; Sodium: 64mg; Carbohydrates: 4.1g; Dietary Fiber: 0g; Protein: 2.8g

WATERMELON COOLER
SERVES 2

With a 92 percent water content and high amounts of vitamin A and cancer-fighting lycopene, it's too bad watermelon isn't available all year round. If you are a fan of this lime-and-fresh-mint-flavored cooler, keep a steady supply of watermelon cubes in your freezer.

2½ cups cubed, seeded watermelon
¼ cup boiling water
1½ tablespoons sugar
2½ tablespoons fresh lime juice
Mint leaves
Lime slices

■ Place the watermelon in a blender or food processor fitted with a steel blade and process until blended. Transfer to ice cube trays and freeze.
■ Place the water and sugar in a cup and stir until the sugar has dissolved. Cover and refrigerate until cool. Transfer to a pitcher, add the lime juice and stir well. Just prior to serving, add the watermelon cubes to 2 glasses and then top with the lime mixture. Serve garnished with the mint leaves and lime slices.

NUTRITION FACTS: Calories: 99; Calories from Fat: 3; Fat: 0.3g; Saturated Fat: 0g; Cholesterol: 0mg; Sodium: 3mg; Carbohydrates: 25.5g; Dietary Fiber: 0.8g; Protein: 1.2g

POMEGRANATE "SANGRIA"

SERVES 1

Although sangria is a Spanish punch made most commonly with red wine, the word *sangria* is derived from the Spanish word for "blood" (referring to its color), so substituting pomegranate juice isn't too far a stretch! I love eating pomegranates, but I have to admit that the popularity and accessibility of pomegranate juice has made it a more commonplace addition to my diet, a good thing considering its health benefits: it has been suggested that pomegranate juice slows aging, protects against heart disease and cancer, increases blood flow to the heart (like exercise) and may lower cholesterol. Drink up!

2½ ounces pomegranate juice
6 ounces brewed black tea
1 teaspoon sugar
¼ peach, sliced
¼ orange, sliced

■ Fill a tall glass with ice cubes, add the ingredients, stir and serve.

NUTRITION FACTS: Calories: 95; Calories from Fat: 1; Fat: 0.1g; Saturated Fat: 0g; Cholesterol: 0mg; Sodium: 3mg; Carbohydrates: 23.8g; Dietary Fiber: 1.5g; Protein: 0.7g

PEANUT BUTTER MILKSHAKE

SERVES 1

Although I have a love-hate relationship with peanut butter, I find myself surrounded by people who seem to thrive on it. Too much will load on the pounds, but this milkshake offers the rich flavor without all the calories. Try this for breakfast as well as for a snack.

1½ teaspoons natural-style peanut butter
½ cup skim milk
1 teaspoon unsweetened cocoa powder
¼ teaspoon vanilla extract
4 ice cubes

■ Place the ingredients in a blender and blend until smooth and frothy. Serve immediately.

NUTRITION FACTS: Calories: 96; Calories from Fat: 39; Fat: 4.4g; Saturated Fat: 1g; Cholesterol: 2mg; Sodium: 89mg; Carbohydrates: 8.8g; Dietary Fiber: 1.1g; Protein: 6.5g

DID YOU KNOW?

JUICE SERVINGS EQUAL TO 100 CALORIES

¾ cup apple juice
¾ cup cranberry juice
⅔ cup red grape juice
1 cup grapefruit juice
⅞ cup orange juice
¾ cup pineapple juice
⅔ cup pomegranate juice
1¾ cup tomato juice

COFFEE-BANANA MILKSHAKE

SERVES 1

I f you're like most people, you brew a pot of coffee only to throw much of it away later in the day. This milkshake is the perfect remedy for wasteful coffee brewing. Fill your ice cube tray with leftover coffee and substitute four coffee cubes for the coffee, or for more coffee flavor, substitute coffee cubes for the traditional ice cubes. It will almost be like a slush!

½ **cup brewed strong coffee, chilled**
¼ **over-ripe banana, sliced**
½ **cup skim milk**
1½ **teaspoons honey**
4 **ice cubes**

■ Place everything in a blender and blend until thick and frothy. Serve Immediately.

NUTRITION FACTS: Calories: 101; Calories from Fat: 2; Fat: 0.2g; Saturated Fat: 0g; Cholesterol: 2mg; Sodium: 55mg; Carbohydrates: 21.5g; Dietary Fiber: 0.8g; Protein: 4.6g

DATE SMOOTHIE

SERVES 1

The richness of the date adds some heft to this tasty smoothie.

⅓ **cup nonfat plain yogurt**
¼ **cup skim milk**
1 Medjool date, pitted
¼ **teaspoon vanilla extract**
4 ice cubes

■ Place everything in a blender and blend until thick and frothy. Serve immediately.

NUTRITION FACTS: Calories: 99; Calories from Fat: 12; Fat: 1.3g; Saturated Fat: 0.9g; Cholesterol: 6mg; Sodium: 83mg; Carbohydrates: 15.1g; Dietary Fiber: 0.7g; Protein: 6.6g

BLUEBERRY SMOOTHIE WITH FLAXSEED
SERVES 1

It's a good idea to add flaxseed to your diet wherever you can. Although it's fattening in large quantities, 1 teaspoon adds only 13 calories but provides more cancer-fighting lignans than almost any other food.

½ cup fresh or frozen unsweetened blueberries
⅓ cup skim milk
2 tablespoons nonfat yogurt
1 teaspoon ground flaxseed
2 ice cubes

Place everything in a blender and blend until thick and frothy. Serve immediately.

NUTRITION FACTS: Calories: 102; Calories from Fat: 16; Fat: 1.8g; Saturated Fat: 0g; Cholesterol: 3mg; Sodium: 57mg; Carbohydrates: 17.4g; Dietary Fiber: 2.4g; Protein: 5.4g

BANANA-COCOA MALTED

SERVES 1

Originally developed as a nutritional supplement for infants, malted milk is made from wheat and malted barley and adds immeasurable flavor to a variety of drinks, most famously those made with ice cream! You can also serve this warm.

¾ **cup skim milk**
¼ **over-ripe banana, sliced**
1 **tablespoon unsweetened cocoa powder**
1 **teaspoon malted powder**

■ Place everything in a blender and blend until thick and frothy. Serve immediately.

NUTRITION FACTS: Calories: 98; Calories from Fat: 10; Fat: 1.1g; Saturated Fat: 0.6g; Cholesterol: 3.6mg; Sodium: 73mg; Carbohydrates: 18.3g; Dietary Fiber: 2.4g; Protein: 7g

KIWI-STRAWBERRY SMOOTHIE
SERVES 1

With even more vitamin C than an orange, the slightly tart/creamy/crunchy kiwi makes a healthy smoothie. Be sure to use only ripe kiwis—their antioxidants increase as they ripen—as the under-ripe ones will ruin your smoothie.

1 kiwi, peeled and sliced
5 fresh or frozen unsweetened strawberries
¼ cup orange juice
1 teaspoon unsweetened shredded coconut
4 ice cubes

■ Place everything in a blender and blend until thick and frothy. Serve immediately.

NUTRITION FACTS: Calories: 99; Calories from Fat: 11; Fat: 1.3g; Saturated Fat: 0.5g; Cholesterol: 0mg; Sodium: 4mg; Carbohydrates: 22.5g; Dietary Fiber: 3.8g; Protein: 1.8g

EGG CREAM

SERVES 1

That there are neither eggs nor cream in an egg cream doesn't detract from its essential goodness. If you haven't tried one, it will certainly sound awful. In the TV show *The West Wing*, the president tries one for the first time and remarks: "I'm drinking the most fantastic thing I've ever tasted in my life: chocolate syrup, cold milk, and seltzer. I know it sounds terrible, but trust me, I don't know where this has been all my life."

½ **cup skim milk**
¼ **cup seltzer**
1½ **teaspoons chocolate syrup (Fox's U-bet is recommended by most aficionados)**

■ Place the milk in a tall glass, add the seltzer and watch the white foam appear. Slowly pour the syrup into the middle of the foam and, using a metal spoon, stir vigorously! Serve immediately.

NUTRITION FACTS: Calories: 96; Calories from Fat: 3; Fat: 0.3g; Saturated Fat: 0g; Cholesterol: 2mg; Sodium: 65mg; Carbohydrates: 18.8g; Dietary Fiber: 0.5g; Protein: 4.5g

DID YOU KNOW?

FRUIT SERVINGS EQUAL TO 100 CALORIES

1 medium large apple
1 small banana
1⅓ cups blackberries
120 blueberries
½ medium cantaloupe
⅞ cup cherries
5 roasted chestnuts
50 grapes
A quarter of a 5½-inch diameter honeydew melon
1 small papaya
2 medium peaches
1 medium pear
100 raspberries
26 strawberries

STRAWBERRY-BANANA SMOOTHIE
SERVES 1

This was my standby smoothie in college, although I started out using orange juice instead of water. Never mind that it had so many more calories: the orange juice makes it too sweet! If you are a fan of smoothies, I suggest you keep sliced over-ripe bananas in your freezer; that way, you will always have a perfectly ripe banana for your smoothie and you can serve it at just the right temperature.

⅓ **cup nonfat yogurt**
⅓ **over-ripe banana, sliced and frozen**
3 fresh or frozen unsweetened strawberries
3 tablespoons cold water

■ Place everything in a blender and process until smooth. Serve immediately.

NUTRITION FACTS: Calories: 98; Calories from Fat: 14; Fat: 1.5g; Saturated Fat: 0.9g; Cholesterol: 5mg; Sodium: 58mg; Carbohydrates: 17.5g; Dietary Fiber: 1.7g; Protein: 5g

MAPLE LEMONADE

SERVES 2

Although I never serve concentrated lemonade, preferring always to make mine from scratch, I am often deterred by how labor intensive it is—specifically, the making and cooling of the simple syrup. I decided to try the faster and more nutritious route of using maple syrup. I now prefer this more subtle and less sweet recipe: the maple seems to mellow the lemon without overwhelming it.

2 cups cold water
½ cup fresh lemon juice
⅓ cup real maple syrup
1 lemon, thinly sliced
Mint sprigs

■ Place the water, lemon juice and maple syrup in a small pitcher or bottle and stir well. Serve over ice with lemon slices and mint for garnish.

Nutrition Facts: Calories: 76; Calories from Fat: 0; Fat: 0.1g; Saturated Fat: 0g; Cholesterol: 0mg; Sodium: 3mg; Carbohydrates: 20.2g; Dietary Fiber: 0g; Protein: 0.1g

PINEAPPLE TEA

SERVES 1

A dding pineapple (and also citrus fruits) to green tea increases many of its benefits, specifically the catechins (found so plentifully in tea), which help to reduce the risk of stroke, heart failure, cancer and diabetes. Pineapple tea can be served either hot or cold.

½ **cup brewed black or green tea, steeped for 5 minutes**
⅔ **cup unsweetened pineapple juice**
¼ **teaspoon grated fresh gingerroot**
⅛ **teaspoon vanilla extract**

■ Place everything in a blender and blend until frothy. Serve immediately.

NUTRITION FACTS: Calories: 101; Calories from Fat: 2; Fat: 0.2g; Saturated Fat: 0g; Cholesterol: 0mg; Sodium: 4mg; Carbohydrates: 24.3g; Dietary Fiber: 0g; Protein: 0.7g

PINEAPPLE-RASPBERRY SMOOTHIE

SERVES 1

Nutritionally speaking, pineapple is most famously touted for containing bromelain, known to help digestion and reduce inflammation. Most of the bromelain is in the stem— which I am happy to claim as my favorite part. In my house, pineapples either get eaten as soon as I return home from the store, or they sit around too long, which is how I developed this recipe; I cut up the pineapple (eating lots of stem while I cut), put half in a container for eating and the other half in the freezer for future smoothies.

⅔ **cup fresh or unsweetened frozen raspberries**
¼ **cup chopped fresh or unsweetened frozen pineapple chunks**
¼ **cup nonfat plain yogurt**
4 ice cubes
½ **teaspoon chopped fresh mint leaves (optional)**

■ Place everything in a blender and blend until smooth and frothy. Pour into a glass and enjoy!

NUTRITION FACTS: Calories: 101; Calories from Fat: 14; Fat: 1.5g; Saturated Fat: 0.6g; Cholesterol: 4mg; Sodium: 44mg; Carbohydrates: 19.2g; Dietary Fiber: 5.9g; Protein: 4.4g

BLUEBERRY–GREEN TEA SMOOTHIE

SERVES 2

This is a two part recipe: first you make the green tea ice cubes, and then you make the smoothie. Don't be tempted to use water ice cubes: the green tea adds an almost lush but subtle flavor that pairs nicely with the blueberries. The green tea also adds lots of health benefits, among them reducing cancer cells, lowering cholesterol, fighting infection and promoting weight loss.

1 cup brewed green tea, cooled
1½ cups fresh or unsweetened frozen blueberries
½ cup plain nonfat yogurt
¼ teaspoon vanilla extract
¼ teaspoon fresh lemon juice
4 to 6 green tea ice cubes

■ Pour the tea into an ice cube tray and freeze.
■ Place the blueberries, yogurt, vanilla, lemon juice and 4 green tea ice cubes in a blender and process until smooth. Pour into 2 glasses and serve immediately!

NUTRITION FACTS: Calories: 102; Calories from Fat: 12; Fat: 1.3g; Saturated Fat: 0.6g; Cholesterol: 4mg; Sodium: 44mg; Carbohydrates: 20.2g; Dietary Fiber: 2.6g; Protein: 4g

MULLED APPLE CIDER
SERVES 4

While you can cheat by using a microwave, mulled apple cider is really at its best after it simmers slowly on the stove. It's well worth waiting for the flavors of spices and citrus to infuse the cider.

3½ cups apple cider
⅛ teaspoon ground allspice
¼ teaspoon ground ginger or cardamom
1 cinnamon stick
Strips from 1 orange peel
Strips from 1 lemon peel

■ Place all the ingredients in a large pot and bring to a boil over high heat. Reduce the heat to low and simmer for 12 minutes. Pour through a strainer and serve or cover and refrigerate for up to 4 days. Gently reheat when ready to serve.

NUTRITION FACTS: Calories: 103; Calories from Fat: 2; Fat: 0.3g; Saturated Fat: 0g; Cholesterol: 0mg; Sodium: 7mg; Carbohydrates: 25.5g; Dietary Fiber: 0g; Protein: 0.1g

HONEY-VANILLA MILK

SERVES 1

This is a wonderful bedtime treat. While the spices are optional, to me they're essential! If you prefer whole milk, simply substitute just under ⅔ cup, or if 2%, substitute ¾ cup.

1 cup skim milk
1 teaspoon honey
¼ teaspoon vanilla extract
Pinch ground nutmeg, cinnamon or cardamom, or more to taste (optional)

■ Place all the ingredients in a small pot and cook over medium-low heat until warmed throughout. Serve immediately.

NUTRITION FACTS: Calories: 105; Calories from Fat: 2; Fat: 0.2g; Saturated Fat: 0g; Cholesterol: 5mg; Sodium: 103mg; Carbohydrates: 17.9g; Dietary Fiber: 0g; Protein: 8.3g

CHOCOLATE SPOONS

SERVES 4

C hocolate spoons—to be added to coffee or warmed milk—are special but cheerfully as uncomplicated as it gets. If you run out of spoons, simply pop the chocolate out of the spoon and store it solo; just prior to serving, return the chocolate to the spoon and let it melt a little bit. Then return it to the refrigerator or freezer. If you don't let it melt and reset it, the whole thing will slide into your drink rather than melt slowly!

4 tablespoons semisweet chocolate chips

■ Line a small plate with parchment paper. Place the chocolate chips in a small microwave-safe container and microwave until melted. Place 4 spoons on the prepared plate, add the melted chocolate chips and refrigerate until hardened.

NUTRITION FACTS: Calories: 70; Calories from Fat: 36; Fat: 4g; Saturated Fat: 2.5g; Cholesterol: 0mg; Sodium: 0mg; Carbohydrates: 9g; Dietary Fiber: 1g; Protein: 1g

INDEX

CROA-TIAN WAR NOC-TURNAL

Phoneme Media
PO BOX 411272
Los Angeles, CA 90041

First Edition, 2017

Copyright © 2017 Spomenka Štimec

Translation © 2016 Sebastian Schulman

ISBN: 978-1-944700-13-3

This book is distributed by Publishers Group West

Cover art by Jaya Nicely
Cover design and typesetting by Jaya Nicely

Phoneme Media is a nonprofit media company dedicated to promoting
cross-cultural understanding, connecting people and ideas
through translated books and films.

http://phonememedia.org

Curious books for curious people.